CONTENTS

Friendships

KEY AIMS: By the end of Part 1, you will:
➢ understand the nature of friendship;
➢ have learned how friendships are formed;
➢ know what causes people to like one another;
➢ understand why we need friends;
➢ know more about the rules and skills of friendship;
➢ be familiar with theories of friendship.

This Unit is about the effect of social relationships on behaviour. The ways in which we behave with parents, with friends and with teachers, for example, are very different. If we can get these relationships right it is very rewarding; if we get them wrong it can cause a lot of distress. Psychologists have found out a great deal in recent years about how social relationships work, and this information is of great practical importance, as well as of theoretical interest.

Very close relationships are formed with people inside the home – between partners, and between parents and children. In a survey in Toronto, Wellman (1979) investigated other relationships, asking people to list 'the persons outside the home that you feel closest to'. The results were as follows.

Table 1.1 (from Wellman, 1979)

	First person named (%)	First 5 people named (%)
Friends	28	38
Siblings	21	15
Parents	19	9
Child	13	6
Neighbours	4	6
Co-workers	3	6

Friends came out top, while neighbours were the weakest relationship, with co-workers as low, though work relationships can be very important, as we shall see.

Friendship has often been assumed by psychologists to be the basic and universal relationship, that of liking and being attracted to another person. We will look at this research, and see what the sources are of this attraction, and how friends are made.

If we ask people what they understand by 'friends', they will say that friends are people outside the family:

• who are liked
• whose company is enjoyed

1

Figure 1.1: Friends are people whose company we enjoy.

- who share interests and activities
- who are helpful and understanding
- who can be trusted
- with whom one feels comfortable
- who will be emotionally supportive.

Males and females see friends differently. Men's friendships seem to be related to shared leisure interests, while women's friendships are more intimate, with women confiding in each other and being emotionally supportive, as Reisman (1981) found in studies of American students. There are other variations with age and social class.

One way of seeing what friends are is by looking at what friends do together. We did this with a sample of Oxford adults, and found that there were a number of distinctive activities which they did more with their friends than with other people. Those activities listed in *Table* 1.2 are all enjoyable leisure activities. They may look trivial, but they may bind friends into supportive relationships. Of course, what these activities are will vary greatly with the group studied. You can probably work out the kind of sample this was.

SOMETHING TO TRY

Make a list of the things you do most often with your friends. Then make another list of the things you do with your family. Can relationships with friends and family be clearly distinguished in terms of these activities?

Table 1.2: Situations/activities most chosen for friendships (ratios to mean frequency for all relationships; Argyle and Furnham, 1982)

	Friend, similar age
Mean ratio for all activities	1.26
Situations above this ratio	
Dancing	2.00
Tennis	1.67
Party	1.63
Joint leisure	1.63
Pub	1.60
Intimate conversation	1.52
Walk	1.50

How many friends do people have?

It depends on who you count as a friend. If we mean 'best friends', the answer may be one or two, especially with adolescents. If we mean 'close friends', it is more like five; 'friends' may come to about 15; and 'acquaintances' to a much larger number – 1,000 in some cases. Another way of counting how many friends someone has is to ask them how many people they count as friends they have seen, or telephoned, in the last week. (No one has studied the role of e-mail in friendship yet.) In a study like this in London, men reported 7.6 friends and women 4.6 friends (Young and Willmott, 1973). But as we shall see later, women have more *close* friends. Some people have no friends at all, or fewer than they would like. Those with the most friends tend to be:

- young (18–25)
- middle class
- single
- extraverts.

How long do friendships last?

Children's friendships change rapidly, but some of those formed during adolescence and early adulthood can last a lifetime. However, friendships change regularly, due to moving house or going to college, changing jobs, or taking up new leisure activities. You will probably notice that your Christmas card list (if you send cards) is somewhat different each year. Friendships last longer for those who:

- are older
- are married and with children
- live near their friends
- are part of a wider network
- are closer.

However, most friendships do not last as long as kinship relations, for example, those between parents and children, or between brothers and sisters, which usually last for ever.

How would you define friendship? List three characteristics of 'friends'.

Where do friends come from?

We are drawn towards others who are similar to ourselves, who have common interests, and whom we see frequently. It is not surprising, therefore, that we make friends with those we meet at school, work, and in leisure groups, but not necessarily with neighbours for example. In a study in London, Willmott (1987) found that the sources of friendships varied with social class.

Table 1.3: Where friends come from (source: Willmott, 1987)

	Middle class	White collar	Working class
Work friends	4.72	3.15	2.51
Childhood or school friends	3.10	1.56	1.34
Friends met through clubs, churches, leisure, etc.	2.68	0.66	1.08
Neighbours who became friends	1.99	1.59	1.80
Ex-university	1.76	—	—

Willmott worked out a very neat piece of statistics from the data in this study, from which it is possible to predict how many friends people will have (see *Table 1.4*). You start at 'Go' with 5.85 friends.

Table 1.4: Predicting how many friends people will have

Basic number of friends	5.85
Further education adds	6.74
Middle class job adds	4.59
One car adds	2.36
Second car adds	2.36

According to this study, middle class people in London had *more* friends, but working class people saw their friends more often. A lot of middle class people's friends come from school or college, from work and from leisure groups. Many surveys have found that middle class individuals tend to belong to more leisure groups, and the type of work they do may be more conducive to getting to know people. Leisure groups, educational institutions and work are all places where we can meet people with common interests. In all social classes, it can be found that some neighbours become friends, though most do not, as we shall see shortly.

Leisure groups, like tennis clubs, religious organizations, and dancing classes, are a very important source of friends, and shared leisure is one of the main things that friends do together. Some kinds of leisure activity produce particularly close friendships. In a recent study I found that belonging to churches and to voluntary work groups often does this, many people saying that these are 'closer than my other friendships' (Argyle, 1996).

What makes people like each other?

Proximity

An important, and simple, reason for liking people is because they live next door, sit at the next desk in school, or work at the next bench. This was shown in a study of American ex-servicemen and their wives at the Massachusetts Institute of Technology (M.I.T.). They were housed in 100 prefabs in an area called Westgate, and 170 apartments in Westgate West, which are shown in *Figure* 1.2.

Couples were asked to name those whom they saw most often socially, and the findings were very striking:

- Couples were 10 times more likely to mention others in the same apartment block as in another block.

- Forty-one per cent named their next-door-neighbours, but only 10 per cent named those at the other end of the building in Westgate.

- Couples were twice as likely to mention other couples on the same floor as on another floor.

- Those couples in the prefabs also mentioned their neighbours, unless their houses faced away from the courtyard and into the street. Those in Westgate whose apartments were at the bottom of staircases knew the people who lived upstairs better. Both these cases were interpreted as

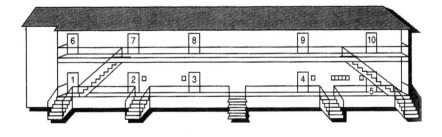

Figure 1.2: Diagram showing the arrangement of one of the married students' apartment buildings at Westgate (Festinger *et al.*, 1950).

5

'functional distance', since it affected how likely couples were to bump into one another.

However, being close to someone can be a source of friction too, and Peter Warr (1965) in a study at Sheffield University, UK, found that being in the same university hall of residence increased the chance of both liking and disliking people, though the effect was much greater for liking.

There have been other studies confirming all this. In one of them, children at school were given seats alphabetically by name, and it was found that proximity strongly affected choice of friends (Segal, 1974). But proximity doesn't work so well with next-door-neighbours. The M.I.T. couples were very unusual neighbours, since they had so much in common – the men were all ex-servicemen, and they were all students at MIT. Most neighbours are much more heterogeneous, differing in age, occupation and so on. As we shall see in the next part of this Unit, similarity is an important factor in attraction, and it seems that proximity is only an influence when people are similar enough.

SAQ 2

When might too much proximity be bad for friendship?

Similarity

It is often found that friends are similar to each other in their beliefs and interests, and in many other ways. But is this because similarity leads to liking, or is it because people who like each other become more similar? The best way to settle these **direction of causation** issues is by experiments. One experimental procedure was devised by Byrne in his **bogus stranger technique**. Participants were given an attitude scale with questions on 26 topics, such as divorce, discipline of children and classical music, each assessed on a six-point scale (see *Figure* 1.3).

Classical Music (check one)

_   I dislike classical music very much.

_   I dislike classical music.

_   I dislike classical music to a slight degree.

_   I enjoy classical music to a slight degree.

_   I enjoy classical music.

X   I enjoy classical music very much.

Sports (check one)

_   I enjoy sports very much.

_   I enjoy sports.

_   I enjoy sports to a slight degree.

_   I dislike sports to a slight degree.

X   I dislike sports.

_   I dislike sports very much.

Figure 1.3: Two of Byrne's items (Byrne, 1971).

Two weeks later the same people were shown a scale supposedly filled in by another participant but actually faked by the experimenter, and were then asked how much they would like to work with this person. The finding was very clear: the greater the proportion of similar attitudes he or she appeared to have, the more participants liked the bogus stranger. This is ingenious and seems to show a direct causal effect of similarity on liking. However, some psychologists feel that this is a very artificial procedure, since there is no encounter with real people.

How valid do you think Byrne's studies were?

Newcomb (1961) carried out a more realistic study. He offered 17 students free accommodation for a term in exchange for filling in his questionnaires. He found that friendship choices developed over the 16-week period, and that those whose attitudes were initially more similar ended up liking each other more than those whose attitudes had been dissimilar from the start. However, this process was slow, perhaps because it takes some time to explore others' attitudes.

Similarity has been found to affect friendship in two main areas – attitudes and values, and leisure interests. Similarity of personality has less clear-cut effects.

There may be situations where similarity doesn't work. Tesser and Campbell (1980) argued that self-esteem may be at risk if another person is similar in ability or performance in areas which are important to the self; we prefer people whose abilities lie in another area. On the other hand, in areas of performance which are not important to our self-esteem we may be able to bask in their reflected glory and will like them more.

What explanation is there for the effect of similarity? There may well be different explanations for different kinds of similarity. A person with similar attitudes or beliefs is liked because they reinforce our own beliefs. A person with similar interests is liked because we can do things together and talk about it, or there may be a universal effect of similarity, which is pleasing in some way.

One way in which this might work was suggested by Aronson and Worchel (1966). They thought that we like those who are similar because we expect *them* to like *us*. They did an experiment which showed that if participants were told that another person liked them, they liked that person back regardless of whether they were similar or not, showing that it was being liked that mattered to them, not similarity.

It has often been suggested that opposites attract – that people can complement one another in various ways. Many studies have been done to try to confirm this, but they have all come up with the same answer: it is similars, not opposites, who are attracted to one another.

SAQ
3

What evidence is there that 'birds of a feather flock together'?

Rewardingness

The third main source of interpersonal attraction is whether the other person is found rewarding. These rewards can be verbal (for example, paying compliments), non-verbal (smiling), or actual practical help. This is such an important factor in friendship that several theories of friendship are based on it, and these are discussed later in this Part (see page 11), together with the evidence for the importance of rewardingness.

Self-disclosure

For people to get beyond a superficial kind of friendship they need to talk about more personal and intimate matters; this is known as **self-disclosure**. Experiments have been done in which participants meet **confederates** in the lab, who disclose either intimate or non-intimate things about themselves. The usual result is that participants are found to like the intimate disclosers more. They also reciprocate by disclosing matters of similar intimacy themselves. Being disclosed to is rewarding, perhaps because it indicates trust and liking, and it is found to be more rewarding to women than to men (Jourard, 1971).

Aron *et al.* (1997) carried out an experiment in which students, initially strangers, were paired at random, and asked to have one of two kinds of conversation. In one condition they were asked to talk for 45 minutes about 36 trivial, 'small talk', topics, such as 'Describe the last time you went to the zoo', or 'Describe the last pet you owned', and in the other condition about 36 more intimate and personal topics, such as 'What is your most treasured memory?' and 'Take four minutes to tell your partner your life story'. At the end of this period, the average rating on various measures of self-reported closeness to the other was 3.25 for the small talk condition and 4.06 for the personal disclosure condition. We shall meet self-disclosure again when we deal with sex differences in relationships, and with problems of loneliness.

Why we need friends

Most people have a strong need to have friends, seeking the company and approval of others, and are unhappy if they are left out or rejected, and are upset by isolation. This is particularly true of young people. Psychologists have located a **need for affiliation**, which can be measured by questionnaires and other psychological tests. It has been found that those with high scores work hard in lab situations at getting to know others (McClelland, 1987). In British studies the personality dimension of **extraversion** has been widely used and is also found to predict sociability, including enjoying meeting new people, going to parties, and trying hard to get to know people. This is often measured by the *Eysenck Personality Questionnaire* (Eysenck and Eysenck, 1985).

However, our social needs include a lot of different desires, such as those for intimacy, co-operation, competition, and dominance. Which ones are most important for friendship? Argyle and Furnham (1983) asked participants to rate their satisfaction with various relationships on 15 scales, each concerned with some form of satisfaction. Statistical analysis found that there were three factors of satisfaction with relationships, as shown in *Figure 1.4*.

- Factor 1 was *material and instrumental help*; friends were an important source of this, though usually less so than a spouse.

- Factor 2 was *social and emotional support*, and here friends were nearly as strong as spouses.

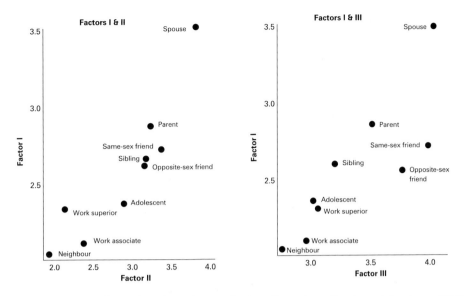

Figure 1.4: Relationships plotted on the satisfaction dimensions (Argyle and Furnham, 1983).

- Factor 3 was *common interests*, that is, companionship, mainly in shared leisure, and here same-sex friends scored as high as spouses.

This study suggests that there are three reasons for having friends – to obtain help; to provide emotional support; and for companionship.

When we come to examine the benefits of relationships we shall see that they correspond to these reported needs.

The rules of friendship

All situations have their **rules**, such as the rule of the road (keeping to the left in Britain), and the same is true of relationships. If you break the rule of the road you are likely to have a collision; does the same apply to breaking the rules of friendship? Will you lose your friends?

We surveyed what people thought about friendship and arrived at a list of things which most people thought friends should and should not do. We then wondered whether these rules were of any importance, whether you might really lose your friends if you broke them. So we asked another sample to think of a friendship which they had lost, and to consider whether this had been caused by either them or the former friend breaking one of our rules. Of course it was more often the friend who had broken the rules! For a number of our rules, breaking them was said to have been important in breaking up the friendship, as shown in *Table* 1.5.

What is interesting and rather surprising about this list is that a number of these rules are about third party relations, such as being jealous, not keeping confidences, and criticizing in public. This tells us something new about friendship; that friends come not one at a time, but in networks, and that it is essential to handle the network skilfully.

An interesting extension of this line of work has been into the **rules of disorder**. Peter Marsh found that apparently unruly football hooligans followed rules of their own, including not actually injuring supporters of the other side,

Table 1.5: Friendship rules and break-up of friendships (Argyle and Henderson, 1985)

	Moderately or Very Important in breaking up friendship	Slightly Important in breaking up friendship
Being jealous or critical of your other relationships	57%	22%
Discussing with others what was said in confidence with him/her	56%	19%
Not volunteering help in time of need	44%	23%
Not trusting or confiding in you	44%	22%
Critizing you in public	44%	21%
Not showing positive regard for you	42%	34%
Not standing up for you in your absence	39%	28%
Not being tolerant of your other friends	38%	30%
Not showing emotional support	37%	25%
Nagging you	30%	25%

but merely humiliating them and making them look stupid (Marsh *et al.*, 1978). Anne Campbell (1981) similarly found that female delinquents followed rules for fighting among women, including not asking your friends to join in, and not calling the police.

SAQ
4

List three reasons why people might need friends.

Friendship skills

It takes some social skills to make friends. We have covered the main ones already:

- *rewardingness*, including being friendly, interesting and amusing;
- *positive non-verbal signals*, smiling and looking, tone of voice;
- *being good at getting to know people*, by self-disclosure, taking an interest in the other person and finding common interests, being good at conversation.

Table 1.6 gives an imaginary conversation between a young man and young woman on a train, scripted by Ellis and Beattie (1976). This illustrates most of the verbal techniques used to establish and enjoy friendships.

SAQ
5

What are some of the skills being demonstrated in Table 1.6? *What is missing?*

SOMETHING TO TRY

You could try out some of these friendship skills on a complete stranger whom you meet at a party or other social occasion and see if you can get to know them.

Table 1.6: A friendly conversation (Ellis and Beattie, 1976)

Scene: train moving through the English countryside: in the compartment sit one man and one woman, both young.	
Man:	Beautiful weather isn't it?
Woman:	Yes, not bad for this time of year.
Man:	Are you going far?
Woman:	To Edinburgh.
Man:	Oh, my brother lives there.
Woman:	Oh, whereabouts?
Man:	Castle Street.
Woman:	Oh, I know it well. I used to have a boyfriend who lived there. But we don't go out any more. Small world isn't it?
Man:	You've got a nice Scottish accent.
Woman:	Thank you.
Man:	What's your name?
Woman:	Zoe – Zoe Purvis.
Man:	Hello Zoe, mine's Ben.

Loneliness

Many people say that they are 'lonely'; 24 per cent of the British population are lonely 'sometimes', 4 per cent of them are lonely 'every day', and this is higher for the young and the old and for women compared with men. An individual's degree of loneliness can be assessed by the University of California at Los Angeles (UCLA) *Loneliness Scale*. *Table* 1.7 has some sample items.

However, a lot of lonely people may have family and friends but still feel lonely. This is because their relationships are not intimate enough; there is not enough self-disclosure (Wheeler, Reis and Nezlek,1983). Others really are isolated and have no friends; some have *never* had a friend. These are the people who probably lack some of the social skills listed on page 10. We will look at ways in which they can be helped later.

However, having friends may not be enough. Weiss (1973) suggested that there are two kinds of loneliness, corresponding to two different social needs. **Emotional loneliness** is felt when there is a lack of an intimate attachment, and **social loneliness** when there is lack of a network of friends or a cohesive group. Later research has confirmed that these two kinds of loneliness are somewhat different, with different effects, and that people need both kinds of relationship (Rook, 1988).

Theories of friendship

Rewardingness

The most common theory of friendship is that it is based on reinforcement, that is, on rewards obtained through the other. An early, and now classic, study

Table 1.7: The UCLA Loneliness Scale (Russell *et al.*, 1980)

	Statement	Never	Rarely	Sometimes	Often
1	I feel in tune with the people around me.*	1	2	3	4
2	I lack companionship.	1	2	3	4
3	There is no one I can turn to.	1	2	3	4
4	I do not feel alone.*	1	2	3	4
5	I feel part of a group of friends.*	1	2	3	4
6	I have a lot in common with the people around me.*	1	2	3	4
7	I am no longer close to anyone.	1	2	3	4
8	My interests and ideas are not shared by those around me.	1	2	3	4
9	I am an outgoing person.*	1	2	3	4
10	There are people I feel close to.*	1	2	3	4
11	I feel left out.	1	2	3	4
12	My social relationships are superficial.	1	2	3	4
13	No one really knows me well.	1	2	3	4
14	I feel isolated from others.	1	2	3	4
15	I can find companionship when I want it.*	1	2	3	4
16	There are people who really understand me.*	1	2	3	4
17	I am unhappy being so withdrawn.	1	2	3	4
18	People are around me but not with me.	1	2	3	4
19	There are people I can talk to.*	1	2	3	4
20	There are people I can turn to.*	1	2	3	4

Note: The total score is the sum of all 20 items.

* Item should be reversed (i.e., 1 = 4, 2 = 3, 3 = 2, 4 = 1) before scoring.

was carried out by Helen Jennings (1951) in an American girls' reformatory. She was trying to find out why so many girls were running away. She found that it was mainly the unpopular ones, and wondered what it was that made some girls popular or unpopular. What she found was that the popular girls:

- helped and protected others;
- encouraged and cheered others up;
- made others feel accepted and wanted;
- controlled their own moods so as not to make others anxious or depressed;
- were concerned with the feelings and needs of others; and
- were able to establish rapport easily, winning the confidence of a variety of others.

This is a very good description of what has come to be called 'rewardingness', which Helen Jennings found was the key to popularity. The unpopular girls on the other hand were dominating, boastful, aggressive, demanded attention, and tried to get others to do things for them – they were trying to get rewards for themselves and incurring costs for others.

We can add a bit more on how to be rewarding. There is a non-verbal side – smiling, looking at the other person, and having a pleasant tone of voice, for example. There is also a verbal side – agreeing, use of first name, humour, paying compliments, and politeness. Verbal and non-verbal aspects of social behaviour are dealt with in a companion Unit in this series, *Social Influence* (Argyle, 1998).

However, rewardingness has some more surprising features. Lott and Lott (1974) arranged for some six- and eight-year-old schoolchildren to succeed at a game four times, receiving a plastic card each time, while playing with two other children. Those who won liked the other two children more as a result – 23 per cent, compared with 6 per cent for the losers. They had not been rewarded by them, merely rewarded in their presence. Other experiments have found that we like people more if we meet them in nice rooms, as opposed to ugly rooms or rooms which are too hot or too cold.

The rewardingness principle can be a useful guide to life, and has been used successfully in therapy. Nevertheless, rewardingness is not the whole story, since other processes affect how much we like each other apart from what we get out of it.

Exchange

Exchange theory is a useful elaboration of reinforcement theory. It was proposed by Thibaut and Kelley (1959) that people constantly try to maximize their rewards and minimize their costs. Therefore, they will choose a friend (or partner) and stay in this relationship if the balance of rewards over costs is as good as they think they can get. The two will both receive rewards from this so they become 'interdependent', and they will reciprocate any good or bad things the other does.

It is proposed that everyone has a 'comparison level for alternatives'; that is, the benefits they might expect to get from other friends. It has been suggested that this theory applies not so much to relations with friends, but to relations with strangers and those in sales or business relations, which have been called 'exchange relations', where people are primarily concerned with doing well out of the relationship.

Communal relationships

Clark and Mills (1979) proposed that there are two quite different kinds of relationships. In **exchange relationships**, people behave like little exchange theorists, and try to maximize their gains. But when in **communal relationships** they behave quite differently and feel some responsibility for meeting the other's needs and are concerned with their well-being and trying to please them. These are close friendships, love, and some family relations.

This theory has been tested by a number of ingenious laboratory experiments, using an attractive experimental accomplice, who seemed to be single and available (the communal condition), or, alternatively, about to be picked up by her husband. In one of these experiments, it was found that in the communal condition the participant would help the confederate, who was in a different room, by sending notes to help her with a task, even when there was no opportunity for her to reciprocate, thus showing a concern for her regardless of possible rewards. In another experiment, it was found that in the communal condition participants did not keep track of their input of help to the other person, but they did keep track of her needs.

These experiments produced the predicted results. However, they are rather artificial, and it is questionable how well they operationalized communal relationships in particular; it sounds more like an embryo dating relationship. In a real-life study, Hays (1985) tried to find out which early student friendships survived by following up a group of students during their first year. He found that rewards *plus* costs was a stronger predictor than rewards *minus* costs, as exchange theory would predict. In other words, these were the friendships where the friends were doing most for each other, thus incurring costs as well as receiving rewards.

It is possible to revise exchange theory to incorporate such findings, by supposing that A feels rewarded, not only by his or her own rewards, but also by a proportion of those received by B. A friend enjoys another friend's pleasure, for example in receiving a gift, or enjoying a meal. This is due to the process of 'empathy', that is, seeing another's point of view, and being concerned about their feelings.

Equity

Another development from exchange theory is the idea that what partners in a friendship are concerned about is not just their rewards and costs, but also with whether they are getting out of the relationship what they deserve, as compared with the rewards received by the other. If people are asked if they feel that they are over-, under-, or equally-benefiting from a relationship, it is of course found that those who think they are under-benefiting are less

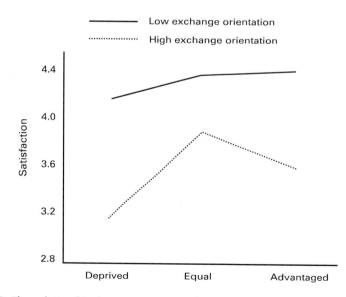

Figure 1.5: The relationship between equity and satisfaction for individuals low and high in exchange orientation (based on Buunk and Van Yperen, 1991).

satisfied with it and are likely to leave. But it has also been found that those who are *over-benefiting* are also dissatisfied; it seems that they feel guilty and prefer fairness. Buunk and VanYperen (1991) found however that this only worked for individuals who had an exchange orientation; that is, who behaved like exchange theorists, and these results are shown in *Figure* 1.5.

When people think they are in an inequitable situation, the theory predicts that they will try to restore equity in some way. It has been found that in marriage they may engage in extra-marital relations, at work they may work less hard.

SAQ
6

What does exchange theory fail to explain?

Which of the findings about friendship do you find most surprising?

SUMMARY

1. Friends are people outside the family whom we like and enjoy doing things with.

2. Friends come mainly from school and college, work and leisure groups.

3. We are most attracted to people whom we see often, and who are similar and rewarding.

4. We need friends since they provide social support, companionship in leisure and instrumental help.

5. To acquire friends requires some social skills; to keep friends we need to keep to the rules.

6. While rewards are important, people are also concerned with fairness of rewards, and, in close relationships, they are also concerned with the needs of their friends.

Other Relationships

KEY AIMS: By the end of Part 2 you will be able to:
➤ *understand the other main relationships – love, marriage, kin and work;*
➤ *recognize the different kinds of bonding involved, and the different activities and rules.*

Romantic love

Falling in love happens to many people, sometimes often. It can be sudden, is usually intense, and can be the greatest source of joy. It is a familiar phenomenon but one which has baffled psychologists. In the modern western world, some people start dating at about the age of 13, but they do not report a love experience until about 17 years of age. Some people engage in what has been called 'serial monogamy', that is, a series of love affairs.

Love consists of powerful feelings of attraction and concern for the other person, and a characteristic set of activities. Dating couples usually spend about a third of their time together if they can. They spend hours together in a combination of increasingly intimate sexual behaviour and increasingly intimate conversation. There is often an increase in conflicts as they get to know each other better, and try to work these disagreements through. They also engage in those joint leisure activities that probably brought them together in the first place.

How do you know if you are in love? You could try filling in the answers on Rubin's *Love Scale*, which is given in *Table* 2.1.

Table 2.1: Love Scale items (Rubin, 1970)

	Love Scale
1	If _____ were feeling bad, my first duty would be to cheer him/her up.
2	I feel I can confide in _____ about virtually everything.
3	I find it easy to ignore _____'s faults.
4	I would do almost anything for _____.
5	I feel very positive towards _____.
6	If I could never be with _____, I would feel miserable.
7	If I were lonely, my first thought would be to seek _____ out.
8	One of my primary concerns is _____'s welfare.
9	I would forgive _____ for practically anything.
10	I feel responsible for _____'s well-being.
11	When I am with _____, I spend a good deal of time just looking at him/her.
12	I would greatly enjoy being confided in by _____.
13	It would be hard for me to get along without _____.

Physical attractiveness plays an important role in love, and has been the object of much research. It can be 'measured' simply by asking two or more judges to rate individuals on a seven-point scale. They will usually agree quite well. The ratings can also be manipulated either by means of clothes, hair and grooming, or more easily by making experimental confederates very unattractive, for instance by means of a wig.

It is widely believed that attractive people possess all sorts of other good qualities; that they are socially skilled, sexually warm, intelligent, sociable, and so on. This is known as the p.a. (physical attractiveness) stereotype. Is there any truth in all this? Studies with students have found that the attractive ones are more popular with the opposite sex, more socially skilled, and less socially anxious, but they are also more self-conscious with the opposite sex (Feingold, 1992). These results are not just from one study but from **meta analyses** in which the results of many studies are combined.

Young people use their appearance in courtship. In a study in 37 different cultures Buss (1988) found that to attract the opposite sex, both males and females:

- keep themselves well groomed and washed, especially their hair
- keep fit
- look healthy
- wear attractive and stylish clothes.

Women attract men by:

- using make-up
- increasing bodily exposure
- wearing sexy clothes.

Men attract women by:

- displaying their muscular strength and athleticism
- talking about their financial prospects and resources.

The biological basis of love

Love is about choosing a mate, which is a very important biological process. To generalize, it has been found that women choose slowly, they go for men who are strong and athletic, and who display signs of assertiveness and say they are rich, who will be able to look after them and their babies, while men go for girls who are young and healthy, have wide hips, and are likely to produce good babies. Females have been found to be more choosy in selecting mates (Kenrick *et al.*,1990). These differing mateship preferences of males and females constitute a part of sociobiology which is widely accepted as applying to humans as well as to animals (Archer, 1996). It is not clear why love can develop so fast; perhaps at some time in our evolutionary history it was necessary to pick mates rapidly or not at all. However, in much of the East, where marriages are arranged by families, love grows much more slowly.

Furthermore, physical attractiveness works, especially in the early stages. In a famous early experiment, Elaine Walster and colleagues (1966) invited 752 new students to a dance where they were paired at random, except that the male was always taller. Ratings of p.a. were made by the experimenters, and this was found to be the only factor which predicted how much each was liked by their partner.

Non-verbal communication is used here, as with making friends, but the signals are different. In addition to smiling and tone of voice, mutual gaze and touch are important (see pages 45–46). A laboratory experiment was carried out in which randomly assorted couples were asked simply to look each other in the eye for three minutes. It was found that ratings of romantic attraction were markedly increased by this experience (Kellerman *et al.*,1989).

The two factor theory of love

Falling in love requires the availability of a suitable and attractive person, usually of the opposite sex. Berscheid and Walster (1978) made an important move in our understanding of attraction and love: they proposed that two further conditions are needed:

(1) a state of physiological arousal; and
(2) labelling this physiological state as love, as the result of social learning.

Almost any kind of physiological arousal will do – loud music, roller coaster rides, a spell on the laboratory exercycle. Dutton and Aron (1974) arranged for a nice looking woman to stop young men in the middle of a dangerous rope bridge at Capilano Canyon in Vancouver to ask them some questions. Fifty per cent of them accepted her invitation to phone her later to hear more about the study, but when the experiment was repeated on a very low bridge only 13 per cent did. They had labelled their anxiety on the first bridge as arousal by the woman.

The other factor is social learning about love, which may come from films and TV or from novels of the Mills and Boon variety. Most young people in the West know about love and what is supposed to happen, but young people who are brought up in parts of India or Japan, where marriages are arranged, will have quite different ideas and expectations, and the same would have been the case in Britain in earlier times. This is perhaps the clearest example of a relationship being, at least in part, a **social construction**, which is shared throughout the culture and is learned during socialization.

SAQ
▽7▽

Under what conditions are people likely to become romantically attracted to one another?

The attachment theory of love

Another theory of love deals with the effect of early relations with parents on later relationships.

John Bowlby (1969) proposed that infants have an innate tendency to become attached to their mother or other main care-giver. This gives an evolutionary advantage, since the infant can seek out this attachment figure when distressed, and can interact with others and explore the environment when she is near. Later research with infants and their mothers found that there are at least three styles of **attachment**:

1 **Secure** – the baby uses the mother as a secure base from which to explore.

2 **Anxious or ambivalent** – if the mother is inconsistent in her behaviour towards her baby, the infant may be anxious or angry when she is close, explore less and cry more.

3 **Avoidant** – if the mother consistently rejects the child he or she will avoid her in strange situations.

It is necessary as adults to end this early relationship with the mother, and to replace it later with a romantic attachment to another. Bowlby thought that these early experiences created a kind of working model of close relationships. Hazan and Shaver (1987) argued that the three styles of attachment are also found for adult attachments. In this and later studies it was found that adult attachment style is similar to that recalled with mothers in childhood.

Relations with the mother in infancy are not the only influence on later love behaviour. It is also found that the child-rearing style of the opposite sex parent affects the child's later relations with the opposite sex. That parent is used as a model of how a romantic partner will be expected to behave, so if this parent was warm and responsive, the child finds it easier to get close to an opposite sex partner. One study showed that males whose mothers were cold or inconsistent tended to date anxious girls (Collins and Read, 1990). No doubt later experiences with the opposite sex also affect the conduct and experience of love, but that would be another theory.

What has been very well confirmed is that those people who experience a high quality of relations with their parents (including discipline) are likely to have a high quality of marriage too, and this has been confirmed in a **meta-analysis** of no fewer than 68 studies (Erel and Burman, 1995).

The course of love

Many people fall in love at first sight, and about 25 per cent of males say they do so by the end of their first date (MORI, 1983); women are much slower and cooler in this matter, choosing more carefully. Often there may be a 'leap of faith'. Murray and Holmes (1997) studied 122 dating couples and 83 married couples. It was found that partners often rated each other unrealistically favourably, for example, as better than average partners, and were unrealistically optimistic about the future of their relationship. When they did so, this caused greater stability in the relationship, and greater happiness. Their initial illusions about each other and about the relationship were confirmed; each came to accept their partner's idealized view of them – a case of a 'self-fulfilling prophecy'.

Several **trajectories** have been found: the course of love may be rapid, but it may also be slow and grow over a long time; it may also be stormy, with several partings and comings together again. This has been shown by studies in which couples are asked to report the history of their relationship from first meeting to marriage (Huston et al., 1981). In a survey of 270 students and 70 workers, Levitt et al. (1996) asked if they had experienced a 'troublesome relationship'. Fifty-six per cent said they had, mainly with opposite sex partners; in most cases the relationship ended because the other was said to be 'selfish, manipulative, demanding'. A strong predictor of this was having had a poor relationship history.

A major cause of break-up is one partner becoming interested in someone else. However jealousy works differently for males and females. It has been found that men are more upset by their partner having sex with another male, while women are more upset by their partner having an emotional attachment to another woman (Buss *et al.*, 1992). This confirms the theory that love is about biology and the production of children – men are worried about who is going to father their partner's children, while women are more worried about the possible transfer of resources to their rival. Jealousy is also partly a matter of self-esteem; DeSteno and Salovey (1996) showed female participants descriptions of possible rivals. Participants said they would feel most jealous if the rival had achieved more than they had in a sphere which was important to them, such as athletics, intelligence or popularity.

SAQ
▽8▽

In what ways does the course of love differ from that of friendship?

What facts should a 'theory of love' be able to explain? Have any of them been successful?

Marriage

Marriage is a very distinctive relationship – the couple usually share their bed, food and property, produce children and care for one another. As *Figure* 1.4 (p. 9) showed, more intense satisfaction is gained from marriage than from any other relationship. A European survey of 160,000 people showed that married people are considerably happier, on average, than single people, those co-habiting, the widowed or the divorced. The results are shown in *Table* 2.2.

Table 2.2: Marital status and happiness (Inglehart, 1990)

	Men	Women
Percentage saying they are satisfied or very satisfied		
Married	79	81
Living as married	73	75
Single	74	75
Widowed	72	70
Divorced	65	66
Separated	67	57

Eurobarometer surveys, *n* = 163,000

It is interesting that the married report being happier than those living together unmarried, and that the divorced are less happy than the widowed. Brown and

Booth (1996), in an American survey of 452 couples who were co-habiting and 1,576 couples who were married, found that couples who were co-habiting had a poorer relationship quality than those who were married. They had more disagreements, fights and violence, and were less happy with the relationship. However, these effects were small, and for those co-habiting who planned to marry there was no difference from the married.

Most people in Britain get married, and nearly 40 per cent later get divorced, the highest rate in Europe, though many divorcees marry again. An increasing number live together without marriage over a long period, though most co-habiting couples marry eventually.

Types of marriage

There are different kinds of marriage in western cultures. The proportion of 'traditional' families, where the husband works and the wife stays at home, has declined greatly since World War II. *Figure* 2.1 shows the American statistics.

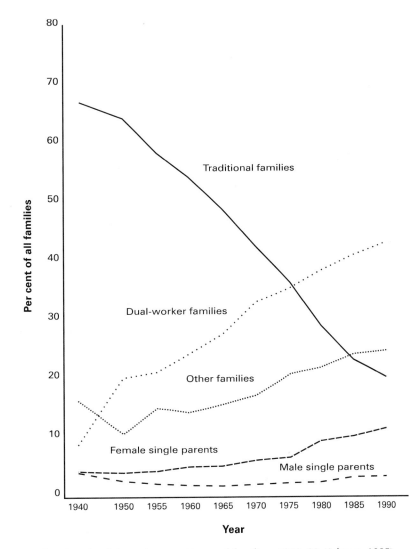

Figure 2.1: The changing labour force patterns of families, 1940–90 (Adams, 1995).

There has been a rise in families where both partners are working, some of them what are termed as 'dual career families' where both work full-time, and in single parent (usually mother) families, as well as more complex families with stepchildren.

In relationships where there is a husband and wife, they may relate to one another in different ways. As well as traditional marriages there are 'independents', who believe in individual freedom and whose relationships have a lot of conflict; and 'separates' who also believe in freedom and who avoid conflict by having less companionship (Fitzpatrick, 1984).

It has often been found that *commitment* is important in marriage, leading to greater marital satisfaction and stability. Bui *et al.* (1996) followed 127 dating couples over 15 years and found that commitment is produced by 'investment', for example, living together, self-disclosure, years of acquaintance and time spent together, and that commitment in turn leads to longer marriages.

Which kind of marriage do you think is most desirable?

Cultural differences in marriage

For many couples in countries such as India and Japan, families play an important role in arranging marriages – love comes later, as was found in a comparison of arranged and love marriages in India. Gupta and Singh (1982) found that the course of love was quite different, and that arranged marriages did better on Rubin's *Love Scale* in the end (see *Figure* 2.2).

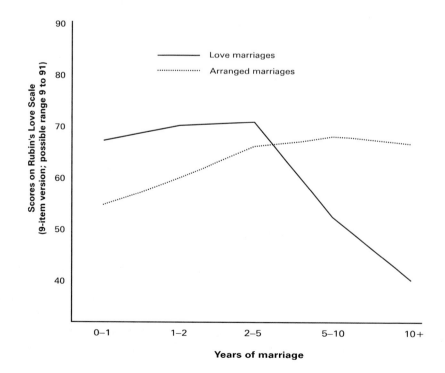

Figure 2.2: Romantic love between partners in arranged or love marriages in Jaipur, India (from Gupta and Singh, 1982).

Traditionally in China men often had a concubine as well as a wife. In Arab culture up to four wives are allowed, for those who can afford them. In Britain there have been major historical changes in the family. The Industrial Revolution saw the growth of the nuclear family, while this century has seen greater equality between husband and wife, many more women working, and the expectation of companionship within marriage.

Within a marriage, the nature of love changes with the years – passionate love is gradually replaced by 'companionate' love, with commitment and intimacy but little passion (Walster and Walster, 1978).

Table 2.3 shows the varieties of activities most commonly shared by married couples and it is interesting that TV has come to be so central to marital life. Shared leisure is important – the more there is, the more likely marriages are to survive. Having rows is also common. In addition, couples share many aspects of their lives which are important sources of satisfaction, such as sex, children, meals together, the home and joint leisure. However, some of these can also be sources of conflict and stress.

Table 2.3: Situations/activities most chosen for marital relationships (Argyle and Furnham, 1982)

Mean ratio	1.64
Situations above this ratio	
Watch TV	2.61
Do domestic jobs together	2.48
Play chess or other indoor games	2.31
Go for a walk	2.28
Go shopping	2.15
Play tennis or squash	2.03
Informal meal together	1.93
Intimate conversation	1.92
Have argument or disagreement	1.84

SAQ
9

What are some of the different forms that marriage can take?

Conflict and divorce

As well as being a great source of happiness, marriage can also be a major source of stress. As mentioned earlier, many marriages break up in Britain, and this is very distressing for all concerned. Marriage is a very difficult relationship: two different people have to live together at close quarters and must come to some agreement over many issues. We found that although spouses are the greatest source of satisfaction to partners, they are also the greatest source of conflict, and as we showed in Table 2.3, having rows was a common marital activity.

Housework is a great source of frustration for many wives. It is found that wives still do most of it, even when they are working full-time, or have exactly the same jobs as their husbands. *Table* 2.4 shows the amount of various household jobs done by husbands and wives in Britain.

Table 2.4: Household division of labour by marital status in Great Britain, 1984

Percentages	Married people Actual allocation of tasks		
	Mainly man	Mainly woman	Shared equally
Household tasks			
(percentage allocation)			
Washing and ironing	1	88	9
Preparation of evening meal	5	77	16
Household cleaning	3	72	23
Household shopping	6	54	39
Evening dishes	18	37	41
Organization of household money and bills	32	38	28
Repairs of household equipment	83	6	8
Childrearing			
(percentage allocation)			
Looks after the children when they are sick	1	63	35
Teaches the children discipline	10	12	77

Source: *Social Trends*, 1986, p. 36.

In addition to the usual rules which are important in relationships, there are some special ones for marriage, of which being faithful, and giving emotional support seem to be the most important (Argyle and Henderson, 1985).

Rewards of marriage

Is sex the secret ingredient that makes marriage so satisfying? During the early months of marriage, many couples have intercourse 3–4 times a week, but this falls to twice a week on average during later years (James, 1983). **Longitudinal studies** have found that sexual satisfaction leads to marital satisfaction, but only for men; for women it works the other way round. As we saw earlier, love is more important for women, because it is seen as a guarantee of future security. Marriage is a close relationship with biological consequences, including the activation of the immune system; close relationships and their associated emotions increase the level of salivary immunoglobulin, part of the immune system, which produces resistance to infection. Marriage can be regarded as a kind of biological co-operative where partners look after one another

We shall see later that training couples in greater rewardingness has been quite successful as a form of marital therapy. It has often been claimed that there is an element of exchange of rewards in marriage; in particular the husband's (usually) greater earning capacity exchanged for the wife's skills and efforts at housework; however, some wives now earn as much as or more than their husbands. Many women are now discontented with the housework–earnings exchange, and would rather go out to work than spend all their time doing housework.

However, another aspect of rewards has been found to be more important than exchange, and that is fairness, or 'equity'; that is, individuals are discontented if they feel they are not getting enough out of the marriage in relation to what they contribute to it, which may include housework, earnings, physical attraction, or social status.

SAQ 10

List three ways in which marriage can be a great source of satisfaction.

Family and kinship

In less developed societies, kinship is the main kind of relationship and it is a central topic in anthropology. Extended families can still be seen in southern Italy and in many other parts of the world. In this section we shall deal mainly with kinship relations outside the nuclear family – adult brothers and sisters, parents and adult children.

Proximity of kin

Some grown-up children still live with their families, even when they are married, mainly for financial reasons. In this case, in western culture, they usually live with the wife's parents, rarely with the husband's. Quite a lot of widowed parents live with the family of one of their children. Often kin live quite near to each other and in one British survey it was found that 69 per cent of over-65s lived near enough to have seen one of their children 'today' or 'yesterday'. In British and American studies it has been found that working class and black families live nearer to each other, and this is because they are not so geographically mobile as other families, who move about because of their jobs and education (Blood, 1972; Morris,1990).

Shared activities

Kin do not usually spend as much leisure time together as friends do, nor do they share as many interests or attitudes. Women in the family may get together to help one another with baby sitting or shopping, and there is a lot of evidence that women keep families together, especially through sister–sister and mother–daughter links – buying presents, providing help, arranging meetings, for example (Allan, 1979; Adams, 1995).

It is kin to whom people turn when they are in trouble and need serious help, rather than to their friends, as Willmott (1987) found in a survey in London, shown in *Table* 5.1 later. Again, it is working class families who help each other more, and this is the result of their closer proximity and more frequent meetings. Working class children often stay at home until they marry, and married couples often live with one set of parents for some time (Morris, 1990). Kin often meet at family gatherings at Christmas and birthdays, not so much to do anything in particular, but to keep in touch and hear the news, and see how children are getting on. There may be many other visits to kin, and if the latter are too far away, many telephone calls.

At Christmas and birthdays it is children and other close kin who get the biggest presents. Kin may provide other kinds of financial help, for grown-up children for example. Property is jointly owned by the nuclear family, and is likely to be inherited by the children eventually. Sisters often borrow clothes, especially children's clothes, and toys, as if these were common property. Money matters are quite different inside families than in the marketplace outside – money is jointly owned and members do not pay each other (Furnham and Argyle, 1998).

The explanation of kinship bonds – sociobiology

Sociobiology is the theory that human behaviour can be explained in terms of evolution – patterns of behaviour are there because they gave some biological advantage to our early ancestors. There are several areas of behaviour for which this approach seems to work. One example is facial expression, which can be traced to our primate ancestors as a social signal. Sexual behaviour is another; it doesn't need to be learnt, and is obviously essential for the survival of the species.

Helping behaviour, altruism and co-operation can also be accounted for, if an extension to Darwin's ideas about evolution is made. This is that the basic biological urge is really for the survival of genes rather than individuals, so that help will be given to all those who share a proportion of our genes. This works well with animals: bees can recognize their close kin by smell and will admit them to the colony; some female birds will help their sisters rather than breed themselves, thus producing more offspring (Dawkins, 1976). So here is a possible explanation of why humans help their kin. Parents and children share 50 per cent of their genes, siblings about the same. These are the kin who give each other the biggest presents, and provide the most help and financial support.

The trouble with sociobiology is that we do not have *clear* evidence that it operates in humans, and there are other possible explanations of what is going on. There is some anthropological evidence however. For example, in the Trobriand Islands men are so promiscuous that they do not know how many of their wife's children they have fathered. As a result, these husbands do not do much for their wife's children, to whom they may not be related, but a lot more for their sister's children, who will certainly share 25 per cent of their genes.

Another theory is that in the early years in the family some kind of emotional learning takes place, perhaps conditioning, which establishes a permanent bond between parents and children and between siblings. This is confirmed by the finding that cousins are more likely to stay in touch with one another if they had been childhood playmates (Adams, 1968).

Yet another theory of kinship is that we are all taught cultural rules, so in Africa a wide range of second cousins and other remote kin are counted as 'brothers', and expect to share any good fortune that comes along. In tribes where the wife has to go and live with the husband's family she will then work for his kin rather than her own. Kinship can be seen as a whole system of rules and relationships, where the whole system has evolved and been found to work. There are many different systems. It may be necessary to marry a certain kind of cousin, to buy the wife from another clan, to avoid the mother-in-law, or to live near the wife's family, for example.

SAQ 11

What proportion of genes do you share with (1) your grandmother (2) a sibling, (3) an uncle (4) a brother-in-law?

SOMETHING TO TRY

If you have cousins, list those you have seen regularly in the last year and those whom you rarely see. Which of the three theories just discussed could explain why the first group are seen more often?

Work relationships

We spend a great deal of time at work, most of it with other people, and this is where many of our friends come from. All kinds of work involve dealing with and relating to other people – colleagues, supervisors or clients, for example. For some jobs, dealing with people is central, as in teaching. A common reason for not succeeding at work is the inability to deal with others.

Work relations are different from all other kinds, in that we have less choice in them; we may have to work with others whether we like them or not. People are brought together by the job, in some kind of **socio-technical system**, where they are linked by the work-flow and the equipment, for example, on an assembly line, in a restaurant, or the crew of an aeroplane.

Work relations are stronger if the work brings people together physically, if they are co-operating on a joint task, if they have equal status, if they share a wage incentive, or if one helps the other. Work relations will be weaker, or even hostile if colleagues are on the opposite side in some way, such as one inspecting the other's work, if there are differences of power or status, or if they have conflicting interests, such as management and unions. These are examples of **role relationships**; that is, the relation depends less on the personalities of the individuals concerned, and more on their place in the social organization (Argyle, 1989).

We can learn more about work relations by seeing what people do together at work. In the following study, we were trying to find out how close these relationships are, since it has been reported that some work relationships, such as those on assembly lines, are very weak, though we also know that many friends come from work. Workers in a fish cannery were asked to report how often they did a range of things with: (1) another worker who had become a friend; (2) another worker who was often seen at work, for example, for coffee, but never outside; (3) another worker whose company was enjoyed but who was never seen for coffee or lunch; and (4) another worker whom they would rather not see at all. The frequencies of different kinds of social activities are shown in *Table 2.5*.

Table 2.5: Frequency of activity according to type of work colleague (Argyle and Henderson, 1985)

| Activities | Mean rating of each work category* | | | |
	Person 1	Person 2	Person 3	Person 4
1 Helping each other with work	4.5	3	2	1
2 Discussing work	5	4	2	1
3 Chatting casually	5	4	3	1
4 Having an argument or disagreement	1	1	1	1
5 Teaching or showing the other person something about work	2	2	1	1
6 Joking with the other person	5	4	2	1
7 Teasing him/her	5	3	2	1
8 Discussing your personal life	4.5	1	1	1
9 Discussing your feelings or emotions	2	1	1	1
10 Asking or giving personal advice	4.5	1	1	1
11 Having coffee, drinks, or meals together	5	3	3	1
12 Committee work, or similar discussion at work	1	1	1	1

*1 = never or rarely; 5 = nearly all the time; 4.5 = collapsed rating of 4 + 5.

It can be seen that in the closer relationships there was more help and discussion of work. What is interesting is the large amount of sociability quite unrelated to work, such as joking, teasing and discussing personal life. Homans (1950) proposed an important theory about this: people come to work to be paid, they discover that there are others there whom they like and so form relationships, for example in chat and games during work breaks. These relationships then feed back into the work, as those who played games together now co-operate over the work.

It is found that there is a lot of this apparently irrelevant fooling about and other sociability; however, cohesive groups also get more work done, and their members have higher job satisfaction; they also provide more social support and help colleagues deal with stresses at work.

The rules for work relationships are different from those for other relationships. They are about doing your fair share of the work, being co-operative, being willing to help, in addition to the third party rules about keeping confidences, and standing up for people in their absence (Argyle and Henderson, 1985).

Should all work groups be given a set period of time for joking and fooling about? What benefits would there be?

SAQ

12

List two ways in which work relations differ from other friendships?

SOMETHING TO TRY

If you do any kind of paid work, keep a list of the different non-work social activities and interchanges which you see over the period of one week.

Supervision

This a universal feature of most work situations – one person is in charge of a group of subordinates. It is a difficult relationship, since the subordinates may resent the supervisor's power to control them and their greater status and pay; the relationship can be more hostile than friendly. On the other hand, some supervisors can be very rewarding, providing social support and solving serious problems for their subordinates.

This was one of the first work relationships to be studied seriously, and the first where objective measures of success have been used. Different supervisors can produce very different levels of productivity; in the case of manual work, some may produce 50 per cent more than others. The effects on rates of absenteeism and labour turnover are much greater, and rates four or even eight times as high may be produced by unskilled supervisors as we shall see shortly.

Classic work on supervisory skills established what has become the standard design for the study of social skills. This procedure was to compare a number of supervisors, in this case 40, whose departments were known to have high productivity, with another 40 whose work groups had low productivity. The skills of the two groups of supervisors were then compared to find out exactly what they were doing that was different (Katz *et al.*, 1951). This is a correlational design, and we now realize that there could be other interpretations of the results, for example, supervisors with good groups supervise differently.

SAQ
13

Why is supervision so difficult?

The power of leaders

Power affects all relationships, but is particularly important at work where there are formal differences in power, in the ability to reward or punish, between supervisors and those supervised. Power could be defined as the capacity to influence other persons, but as generally used it is the capacity to influence people whether they want to be influenced or not, for example by coercive methods.

Power in organizations depends mainly on formal positions of leadership, but these leaders have to have their authority 'legitimized'; that is, they have to be accepted as leaders by their subordinates. There is also *informal* power in organizations and elsewhere, for example, that of some secretaries.

Six different kinds of power were distinguished by Raven *et al.* (1980), and this usage has been widely followed. These are:

1. *Coercive* power, from the ability to punish;

2. *Reward* power, from the ability to reward;

3. *Legitimate* power, when the recipient accepts the influencer's right to give orders, and his own obligation to obey them;

4. *Referent* power, when the recipient wants to be like the influencer;

5. *Expert* power, when the recipient recognizes the superior knowledge, ability or expertise of the influencer;

6. *Informational* power, when the influencer has greater knowledge.

Etzioni (1961) argued that different organizations use different kinds of power. Prisons and mental hospitals use coercive power, industry uses reward power, in the form of wage incentives, while universities, churches, hospitals and voluntary organizations control their staff by what we are now calling legitimate power, by appealing to their motivation and commitment to the shared goals.

In another Unit in this series, *Social Influence* (Argyle, 1998), we discuss the phenomena of *conformity* and *obedience*. It is argued there that conformity in groups depends on two kinds of power, *normative power*, which is really the power of members to reward and punish by social approval and disapproval (our coercive and reward powers), and *informational power*, where the judgements of other members are taken as a source of information. Obedience in military and some other organizations depends on coercion, and fear of punishment, but in Milgram's famous experiments (1974), obedience was based more on legitimate power.

There has been a lot of interest in power in medical settings; for example, how to enforce procedures in hospital which will prevent the spread of infection. Raven and Haley (1980) carried out a survey of medical personnel and asked them which kinds of power would be most likely to affect their behaviour in this matter: they found that expert power was thought likely to be most effective.

Doctors sometimes try to influence patients by using expert power, as in this example of a mother whose baby had a heart murmur.

> Doctor: Watch your Coomb's titres.
> Mother: Oh. Yeah.
(Korsch and Negrete, 1972)

This of course did not have much effect, as it wasn't clear what the doctor meant, and in any case patients are more likely to internalize any recommendations if they feel they have some personal control, as for example with referent power, rather than with coercive, expert or reward power (Rodin *et al.*, 1979).

What is the effect of power? The most obvious effect is that powerful people (by definition) are able to influence others, often against others' will. Laboratory studies have found that the low-power members of groups also imitate powerful members (indicating referent power), and that they are the centre of attention and recipients of many communications. On the other hand, using power, especially coercive power, weakens the relation between a leader and his or her followers; they are no longer in a co-operative, participatory relationship. And low power members may find ways of increasing their power over such a leader, by forming coalitions, as with trade unions, by withdrawing from the relationship so that the leader becomes dependent on them, or by creating group norms which the leader has to recognize or conform to (Hollander, 1985).

Summary

1. Love is a more intense version of friendship, with an added ingredient, producing sudden attachment and great arousal but also care for the other.

2. Marriage is the most intense and rewarding relationship, with attachment similar to that between parents and children, partly because of the sexual rewards. There is a lot of division of labour, the nature of the relationship changes over time, and there is great distress when it is ended.

3. Other kin are seen less often than friends, but are called on for serious help, given large presents, and these relationships are enduring; this form of attachment may be partly due to the sociobiological theory of concern for those who share our genes.

4. Work relations are based on role relations and the organization of work, but positive relations develop between some work colleagues, producing job satisfaction and co-operation over work. Supervision needs special social skills, and depends on the use of power, of which there are several kinds: *coercive, reward, legitimate, referent, expert,* and *informational.*

The Benefits and Costs of Relationships

KEY AIMS: By the end of Part 3 you will:
➤ *have learnt about the various benefits and costs of different relationships, for happiness, mental and physical health;*
➤ *be familiar with the research methods used to investigate these benefits and costs.*

All positive relationships produce benefits for happiness, mental health and bodily health. Combined measures of social support from a range of relationships give a correlation of 0.50 with happiness. The effect of satisfaction with different relationships on happiness was found in a big American survey, as shown in *Table* 3.1. Note that while financial situation has the highest average rating, family life has a higher regression coefficient, that is, covaries more with satisfaction.

Table 3.1: Sources of satisfaction in everyday life (from Campbell, Converse and Rodgers, 1976)

	Mean importance rating	Regression coefficient
Family life	1.46	0.41
Marriage	1.44	0.36
Financial situation	2.94	0.33
Housing	2.10	0.30
Job	2.19	0.27
Friendship	2.08	0.26
Health	1.37	0.22
Leisure activities	2.79	0.21

These numbers are **regression coefficients**. What they show is the extent to which each factor is an independent source of satisfaction. The larger the figure between 0 and 1, the greater the effect of each variable. The figure of 0.41 for family life satisfaction indicates quite a strong effect here, if we assume that it is satisfaction with family life which is affecting life satisfaction, rather than vice versa. These results are consistent with one of the studies mentioned earlier which showed that marriage had a strong effect on satisfaction, followed by relationships with friends and work-mates (Argyle and Furnham, 1983).

The effect of relationships on joy

An important part of happiness is joy, or being in a good emotional state. Positive emotion can be measured on a seven-point scale of joy, from 0 for 'absence of joy' to 7 for 'intense joy', for a particular moment, or averaged over recent weeks, for example, by 'What is your state of joy at the end of a typical meeting of the club?' (Argyle, 1996).

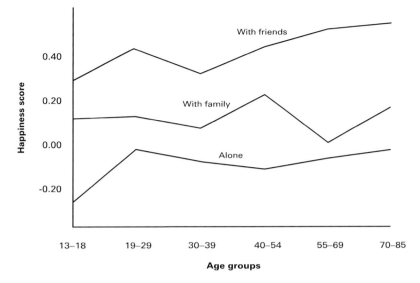

Figure 3.1: Positive affect with different companions (from Larson, 1990).

The greatest source of joy is being in love. One reason for this is that being in love, and being loved, enhances self-esteem. Aron *et al.* (1995) used a 'high risk' method, using first year students thought to be at risk of falling in love. Out of 325, 108 did so in the first term, and it was found that these students experienced changes in their self images, increased in self-esteem and in reported self-efficacy, each assessed by a series of self-rating scales.

Being with friends is also found to be a common source of joy. Larson (1990) used a 'bleeping' method, in which participants were paged on random occasions and then filled in scales saying who they were with and how happy they were (see *Figure* 3.1).

It can be seen that most people were happiest when with friends, followed by being with family. The benefits of being with friends were greatest for the young and the old. A study of students in five European countries asked which occasions produced most joy. The most common was being with friends (36 per cent), followed by eating, drinking, sex and experiences of success (Scherer *et al.*, 1986).

Why does being with friends cause so much joy? We have seen that friends do very enjoyable things together (*Table* 1.2). It is also found that friends smile at each other a lot, expressing affection, a further source of pleasure and self-esteem.

Satisfaction and enduring happiness
If we look at more enduring measures of happiness, marriage has the greatest effect. Surveys have found that the married are considerably happier, on average, than the single, those co-habiting, the widowed or the divorced, in that order (*Table* 2.2). We saw earlier that marriage in particular provides several benefits, including material help, emotional support and companionship. Evidently just being married helps, but being *happily* married is even better, as other studies have found.

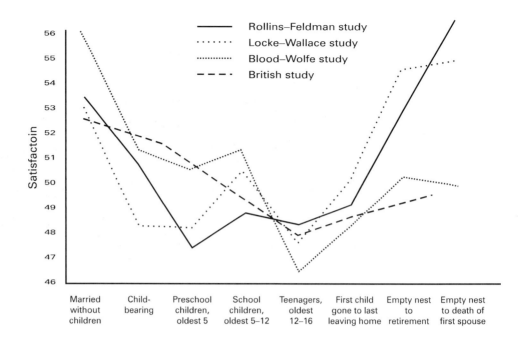

Figure 3.2: Marital satisfaction and the life cycle (Walker, 1977).

Children can be a great source of happiness. Hoffman and Manis (1982) found that 63 per cent of American parents valued the affection, 58 per cent the 'stimulation and fun', while some talked about the 'expansion of the self', or self-fulfilment, or the sense of achievement. Children can also cause a great deal of unhappiness to parents, at certain points in the family life cycle, as *Figure* 3.2 shows. Marital satisfaction in these studies was on average quite low when the children were under four and when they were adolescents.

Happiness correlates with number of friends, frequency of seeing them, going to parties and dances and belonging to teams and clubs. However, there is always a doubt about these correlational findings. Does having friends cause happiness, or do happy people find more friends? There have been several experiments to test this, where one group of people is persuaded to find new friends, increase participation in clubs and leisure activities, and start dating someone, for a month. This led to higher measures of happiness, and even to fewer psychiatric symptoms. These individuals were students and it is not reported how much their work suffered with all this extra social life (Reich and Zautra, 1981)!

Do you think ethics committees should approve experiments such as that just mentioned?

Belonging to leisure groups is an important source of friends as we have seen, and this is an important route to happiness, for the simple reason that leisure is under our own control. Changing your spouse, job or personality is rather difficult, while changing your leisure is very easy. We carried out a study of several hundred mainly young people who were asked to report their mood at the end of a typical meeting of various leisure groups. The results for 'joy' are shown in *Figure* 3.3.

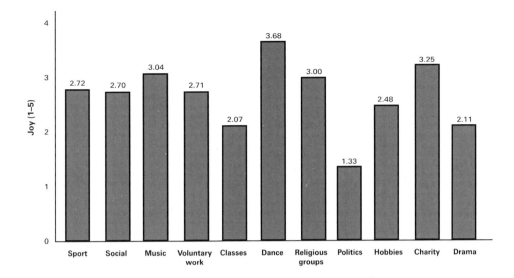

Figure 3.3: Ratings of joy at end of meeting (from Argyle, 1996).

Dancing apparently produced the most joy, followed by charity work, music and religious activities.

Work relations are important sources of happiness too. Winstead *et al.* (1995) studied 722 faculty and staff at an American university. An important source of job satisfaction was found to be the quality of the relationship participants had with their best friend at work. Other studies have shown the importance of belonging to cohesive work groups for job satisfaction, and the resulting lower absenteeism and labour turnover (Argyle, 1989).

Can relationships make us unhappy? Clearly they can when they go wrong. The greatest source of unhappiness here is when a relationship is lost, through death, divorce or separation. We have seen some of the effects on happiness, for example in *Table* 2.3. Unhappiness can also come about through conflict – quarrels between lovers, between husband and wife or between parents and teenage children. We shall discuss what can be done to alleviate such conflicts later.

SAQ
14

In what ways can relationships make people happy?

SOMETHING TO TRY

Make up seven-point self-report scales for Happiness, Depression and Anxiety. For example:

   not happy _____ very happy

Participants mark how they feel with a cross, which is scored by measuring its distance from the left-hand end of the scale. Give them to a number of individuals before and after going out with friends. Predictions: participants will report feeling happier and less depressed and anxious after seeing friends.

The effect of relationships on mental health

Relationships do more than enhance happiness; they can make people less anxious and depressed and less likely to need psychiatric treatment. Mental health can be assessed in a psychiatric interview, or in big surveys by a questionnaire, like the *General Health Questionnaire*, which contains items such as 'Have you recently lost much sleep over worry?', and 'Have you been feeling unhappy and depressed?'.

Brown and Harris (1978) interviewed a sample of working class women in south London. They found that those who had husbands or partners who acted as confidants were much less likely to be depressed as the result of stressful life events (see *Table* 3.2).

Table 3.2: Depression, stress and social support (% depressed) (from Brown and Harris, 1978)

	Support		
	High	Mid	Low
% women who had stressful life event	10	26	41
% women with no such events	1	3	4

This is called a **buffering** effect: social support is useful when there is stress, otherwise you don't notice it much. This has been compared to the effects of sun-tan oil, which only works when one is exposed to the sun.

The social support of family can have other powerful effects, such as keeping us out of mental hospitals. Cochrane (1988) found massive differences between the rates of mental hospital admissions, especially between the married and the divorced, for both men and women (see *Table* 3.3).

Table 3.3: Mental hospital admissions and marital status (England, 1981; Cochrane, 1988)

Marital status	Mental hospital admissions per 100,000
Single	770
Married	260
Widowed	980
Divorced	1437

A weakness of these marriage studies is that the results simply show correlation between variables; they could be due to mentally disturbed individuals being less likely to get married, or finding other sources of social support. Horwitz *et al.* (1996) got round this by studying 340 individuals who got married, and 482 who remained single, over a 17-year period. For those who married there were changes to lower average levels of depression and alcoholism. There was also some reverse causation, in that women who were initially depressed were less likely to get married. And we have seen that joy is very high when people are

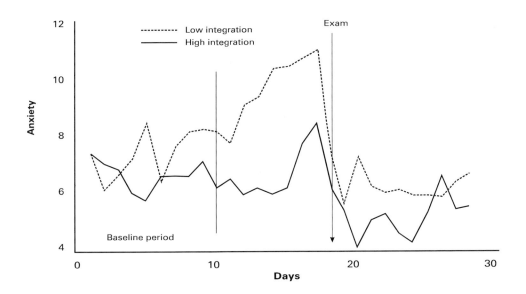

Figure 3.4: The effects of social support on examination anxiety (from Bolger and Eckenrode, 1991).

first married (*Figure* 3.1), and that those who become divorced or widowed are very unhappy for a time, so that it is clear that marriage can have a causal effect on mental health.

We have only mentioned marriage so far, since this has the greatest effect on mental health. Friends also help. Bolger and Eckenrode (1990) found that students were made much less anxious during the period of examinations if they had friends among the other students (see *Figure* 3.4).

Loneliness is an important cause of depression and, as we have seen, can be in part due to lack of social skills. In fact, poor social skills are an important factor in mental disorder, because they result in lower levels of social support. For example, Sarason and Sarason (1985) found that those who had poor social support had rigid, authoritarian attitudes, with little tolerance for deviance, and a negative, alienated and pessimistic view of life. In an American survey of 3,300 adults, Von Dras and Siegler (1997) found that those who earlier had been found to score high on extraversion, at mid-life engaged in more social activity and thought that they had plenty of social support available to them if they needed it.

Work colleagues also help to buffer stress. There may be a lot of stress at work, such as carrying out dangerous work, having unpleasant physical conditions, physically demanding work, difficulties with staff members, boredom, or the amount or rate of work demanded. These and other aspects of work can make people mentally disturbed, suffering anxiety, depression, burn-out, or psychosomatic bodily symptoms, together with heart attacks and ulcers. It should be mentioned that some people do prefer exciting and demanding work – we all have our preferred level – but it is when the job is too demanding that we get ill.

However, social support at work can prevent such illnesses happening. *Figure* 3.5 shows the results of a study by House (1981) of the effects of three kinds

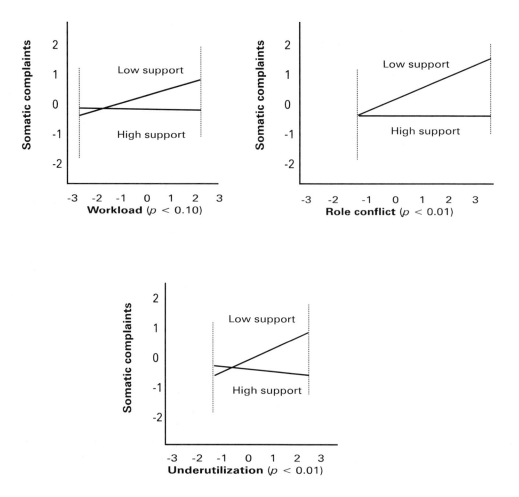

Figure 3.5: Buffering effects of co-worker support on relationships between perceived job stress and somatic complaints (adapted from House, 1981). Note: dotted lines delineate highest and lowest observed values of perceived stress variables.

of work stress on ulcers and neurotic symptoms for those who did and did not have social support from various sources.

The greatest effects came from support from the working group and supervisor, while spouses had rather less effect – he or she can't do much about what happens at work.

What is meant by 'buffering'?

How do relationships help mental health?

But how exactly do relationships relieve the effects of stress? The Brown and Harris study suggests that having a sympathetic confidant is the key, rather like having an amateur psychotherapist in the home. And we saw before that to avoid loneliness it is necessary to be able to talk to friends about personally important topics. Pennebaker (1989) found that if people were able to talk for five minutes about upsetting events, such as seeing a friend being killed, even if they only talked into a tape recorder, their visits to the doctor were much reduced. Other studies suggest it is really love, that is, a close relationship, as in marriage, which affects the immune system. Other studies suggest that companionship is more important – enjoying taking part in joint leisure activities together for example – or it may be that feeling accepted and loved is what is important.

When relationships have negative effects

There can be costs to relationships too. We saw that marriage is a potentially major source of conflict as well as of satisfaction, and we have just seen that the divorced have a very high rate of mental hospital admission (*Table* 3.3). It is interesting that marriage in particular can be the source of both massive rewards and punishments. One ingenious measure of marital satisfaction is simply to record the frequency of sexual intercourse minus the frequency of door-slamming rows. Marital rows can do worse than slam doors; there can be physical violence too.

We saw in *Figure* 3.2 that there are bad as well as good periods of family life. One fairly bad period, for wives at least, can be when there are infants in the home. Brown and Harris (1978) in the study cited found that this was a strong predictor of depression in women, particularly working class women.

Having adolescents in the home can also be difficult for parents, as *Figure* 3.2 also showed. Rows with adolescent children can do more than make their parents unhappy, they can lead to the end of the marriage, with its consequences for poor mental health.

The effect of relationships on physical health

Health is an important aspect of well-being. It is hard to measure, and requires a physical examination and interview. This has often been done, but there is an even better measure which has also been used – just staying alive.

Many illnesses are partly caused by stress. For example, heart attacks are partly caused by arousal of the sympathetic nervous system under stress, which increases the heart rate and blood pressure. Some cancers may be partly due to suppression of the immune system. People who have had recent stressful events are more likely to catch colds than others. However, social support from other people can counter these effects of stress. In a famous study in California (Berkman and Syme, 1979), 6,900 individuals were followed over nine years. At their first testing, many things were measured, including their health and the strength of their supportive networks – family, friends, and organizations such as religious bodies. The participants were left for nine years and the second measure was simply how many of them were still alive. Considerably more of those with the stronger social networks were still alive, as is shown in *Figure* 3.6.

For example, look at the graph for men and at those initially in their 50s; only 9.6 per cent of those with strong social networks had died, compared with 30.8 per cent of those with the weak networks. This has been repeated in many later studies.

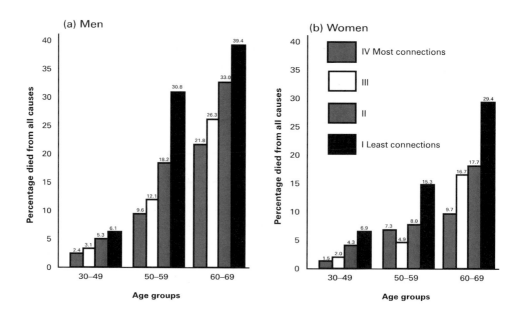

Figure 3.6: Social networks and mortality (Berkman and Syme, 1979).

Table 3.4 shows the results from another study, this time giving the death rates for white males in the USA from the main fatal diseases. It shows deaths per 100,000 over a two-year period for males between the ages of 15–64, with age held constant between married and the other categories. Take the first line, which shows that 362 per 100,000 of the divorced men died, compared with 176 of the married. There are similar differences for other illnesses.

Being *happily* married is even better for health. Wickram and Elder (1997) studied 364 married individuals in the rural mid-West of America over a four-year period. The initial level of quality of marriage, and changes in this, both predicted physical health, as well as happiness and the absence of depression or other kinds of psychological distress.

What is the reason for this apparent advantage of being married? It is found that married people engage in better **health behaviour**, such as drinking and smoking less, having a better diet, having vaccinations and check-ups and generally doing what the doctor orders. However, there is more to it than this. Families look after one another; they share food, bed and illnesses and are concerned about the welfare of the others. There is a second reason. Those who are in a close relationship have more active **immune systems**, since these are responsive to the emotions produced by close relationships (Kennedy *et al.*, 1990).

Friends have less effect than marriage on health, but close relations between students have been found to be related to fewer visits to the doctor. Religious affiliations also have positive effects, partly no doubt because of the close social support already described, but also because of better health behaviour. The greatest effects on health have been found for churches with strict health behaviour codes, like the Mormons and Seventh Day Adventists (Jarvis and Northcott, 1987).

Table 3.4: Marital status and mortality: males (from Carter and Glick, 1970)

Cause of death	Death rates for white men			
	Married	Single	Widowed	Divorced
Coronary disease and other myocardial (heart) degeneration	176	237	275	362
Motor vehicle accidents	35	54	142	128
Cancer of respiratory system	28	32	43	65
Cancer of digestive organs	27	38	39	48
Vascular lesions (stroke)	24	42	46	58
Suicide	17	32	92	73
Cancer of lymph glands and of blood-making tissues	12	13	11	16
Cirrhosis of liver	11	31	48	79
Rheumatic fever (heart)	10	14	21	19
Hypertensive heart disease	8	16	16	20
Pneumonia	6	31	25	44
Diabetes mellitus	6	13	12	17
Homicide	4	7	16	30
Chronic nephritis (kidney)	4	7	7	7
Accidental falls	4	12	11	23
Tuberculosis, all forms	3	17	18	30
Cancer of prostate gland	3	3	3	4
Accidental fire or explosion	2	6	18	16
Syphilis	1	2	2	4

Death rates per 100,000

List some possible reasons why relationships are good for physical health.

Bereavement

We saw earlier that it definitely seems to be bad for the health to be widowed. Not only are the widowed single, but they have also experienced a severe loss. The loss seems to be greater for those who are widowed when young, as *Table 3.5* shows.

The most common cause of death is heart attacks. Lynch (1977) gave the inspired title of *The Broken Heart* to his book on this subject, which showed that loss of a close relationship increases the death rate, particularly from heart attacks.

We referred earlier to the theory that there are two kinds of loneliness, that due to lack of an intimate relationship and that due to lack of a network of friends. The bereaved have lost an intimate attachment; can the other kind of relationship compensate for this loss? Stroebe *et al.* (1996) studied 60 recently widowed and 60 married individuals, and found that the bereaved scored higher on the *Beck Depression Inventory*, and that having a network of family or friends did not make any difference. This is a rather surprising result, and needs further investigation. This gives some confirmation to the idea that there are two kinds of loneliness.

Table 3.5: Death ratios for widowed versus non-widowed men and women in various countries. A ratio above 1.00 means that more widowed died than those living with a spouse. (Adapted from Stroebe *et al.*, 1987.)

Country	Sex	Death ratios by age (years)		
		35–44	45–54	55–64
United States	Men	2.9	2.0	1.5
	Women	1.8	1.4	1.2
England	Men	2.8	1.9	1.6
	Women	2.3	1.5	1.4
Germany	Men	4.2	2.5	1.8
	Women	2.2	1.6	1.3
Japan	Men	4.5	2.9	2.0
	Women	1.6	1.4	1.3

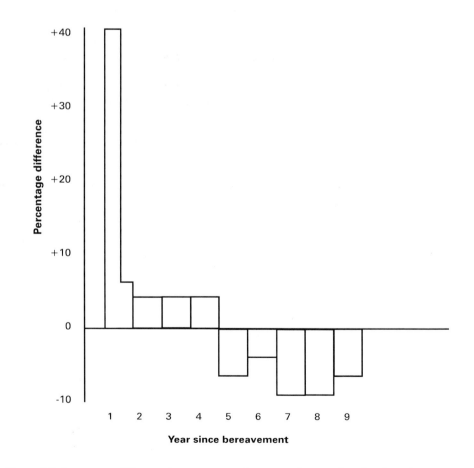

Figure 3.7: Percentage difference between mortality rates of married and widowed men over 54 by years of bereavement (from Young *et al.*, 1963).

However this period of distress is temporary for most, partly because many of them marry again. *Figure* 3.7 shows the increased death rates for men and women at different periods after the death of a spouse.

It can be seen that for men the first six months are the worst, perhaps because of their domestic situation, having to manage the cooking, children and so on. Men do not have such good social support outside the home – their wife is often the main source – while women have more female friends and relations whom they confide in. For women the worst period is the second year of bereavement, perhaps because their worst problems are financial ones which may not become apparent immediately.

SAQ 17

Give three reasons why bereavement is so distressing.

Think of some groups of individuals who might be expected to have health which is better or worse than average as a result of social factors.

Summary

1. Relationships can be a major source of happiness.

2. Close relationships are important for mental health; they buffer stress, but can produce negative effects when they go wrong or when they are lost.

3. Close relationships are good for physical health, partly via better 'health behaviour', partly through strengthening the immune system.

4. Early studies were correlational, giving doubts about the direction of causation; however, recent studies have been able to demonstrate the causal effect of, for example, getting married.

Success and Failure with Relationships

> KEY AIMS: By the end of Part 4 you will be able to:
> ➤ discuss what research has found about the social behaviour which leads to success or failure with friendship and other relationships;
> ➤ understand how such findings are obtained;
> ➤ see how social skills can be trained.

Friends

We have seen that everyone needs friends, since they are a source of happiness, companionship and other aspects of social support. Those who do not have many friends feel lonely and depressed. This is a very common situation, especially for the young, and methods of social skills training have been devised with this group in particular in mind.

Social skills training (SST) is done basically by **role-playing**. That is, trainees try out a certain skill with other trainees acting as 'stooges', and are then shown how to do it better. This is usually done in small groups. The procedure has three steps, as follow.

1. A particular skill is explained and demonstrated; for example, how to start a conversation, how to use positive non-verbal signals. This can be done by the trainer or by showing a video.

2. Each trainee has a go, for 5–8 minutes, with one or two other trainees as stooges, and this is video-taped.

3. After each performance the trainer gives feedback, making constructive comments on the performance, and showing the video. The other trainees watch and join in the discussion of each performance; studying others' performance is part of the training.

A number of sessions is needed, and serious training generally uses video cameras, a one-way screen and a lab. However, a lot of training can be done without all this equipment.

It is necessary to show that SST works, and this is done by comparing the performance of trainees before and after the training. Ideally there should be a control group of similar individuals who have an equal amount of attention paid to them and who are given the before and after measures, but no social skills training. The social skills of trainees can be assessed before and after by seeing them in action or obtaining ratings on their real-life performance. Objective measures can be taken of work performance, like output or sales, or in other cases, the number of dates. There have been many such follow-up studies, most of them showing positive results.

Role-playing can be augmented by other methods. Training in non-verbal communication is one, helping with self-presentation another. A certain amount can be done by normal educational methods, for example explaining the rules which should be followed, or explaining what friendship involves. One study of

44

adolescent girls with no friends found that they had an inadequate and rather childish concept of friendship, and did not realize that it involved commitment and concern for the other person.

Here are possible themes for these sessions.

- Conversational moves
- Rewardingness
- Being assertive and co-operative
- Positive non-verbal signals
- Taking the role of the other
- Self-presentation
- Self-disclosure

Further details of these friendship skills can be found in Argyle (1994a).

Can you suggest some ways that would help a person with few friends go about changing the situation?

How to keep friends

After making friends the next step is to keep them. We have seen that rewardingness is important, and we have seen that the rewards only have to occur in our presence – we don't necessarily have to provide them. It is sufficient to have regular meetings under enjoyable conditions, such as dancing, tennis, or other leisure activities.

A common way of losing friends, as we saw, is breaking certain important rules of friendship, especially 'third person' rules, like keeping confidences, and standing up for friends in their absence.

Love and courtship

This has a lot in common with making friends, but with some important differences. However, it is found to be much more difficult by many young people, and some do not succeed at all. The problem seems to be that although opposite sex situations are more arousing, they may also cause a lot of anxiety.

A proportion of students report great anxiety or avoidance over meeting the opposite sex, rather a large proportion at the time of our 1981 study: 35 per cent of a sample of Oxford students said they would have 'moderate or severe difficulty' in going to a dance or disco, and 26 per cent in going to parties (Argyle *et al.*, 1981). This was in their second year; in their first year the figures were much higher.

The social signals and skills involved are the same as for friendship, but with some extra ones. These are partly non-verbal:

- touch is of central importance, at first on the hand and later in areas of increasing intimacy;

- gaze, leading to mutual gaze, and also pupil dilation, though this is not under conscious control;

- appearance, including grooming and washing, especially of the hair, and for females some degree of bodily exposure; we have seen that males display their bodily strength;

- smiling, head-nodding and an alert body posture also send the right signals.

Verbal skills are important. It was found that young American males who were successful in dating girls were more fluent at saying the right thing, and quickly, and agreed more (Arkowitz *et al.*, 1975). Again, searching for common interests and shared attitudes, and taking an interest in the other person are needed. We gave an example earlier of an imaginary conversation between a young man and young woman on a train, which illustrated some of these skills (*Table* 1.6). As they get to know each other better, another problem is common. With a rapid increase of intimacy and greater self-disclosure couples frequently discover things which they disagree over. If the relationship is to develop they have to work through these disagreements, and come to some compromise. Unresolved disagreements cannot just be left on one side as they can with less intense relationships.

SAQ
19

List some verbal and non-verbal skills useful for courtship.

Marriage

We have already noted the high rate of divorce in the western world – about 40 per cent of marriages in Britain end in divorce. There is also a lot of conflict between those who remain married, and an American study found that 28 per cent of spouses had experienced physical violence from their partners (Straus *et al.*, 1980). The costs of marital failure are immense, psychological as well as economic, and worse than bereavement for the ensuing effects on health, mental health and happiness. It can have enduring effects on any children from the marriage.

What is done differently in happy marriages? This may lead us to the skills needed. Many studies have compared happy and unhappy marriages, and here are the main characteristics of a happy marriage:

- Many positive and rewarding verbal acts, such as compliments and few negative ones, such as criticisms.

- Many positive and rewarding non-verbal acts, such as touches, kisses, presents and help, and few negative ones such as grunts of disapproval.

- Shared leisure activities.

- Enjoyable sex life.

- Settling disagreements by discussion, problem-solving and compromise, rather than by violence.

- Keeping to the rules of marriage, of which the most important is 'Be faithful'.

- Confirming the spouse's self-image.

- Supporting the spouse's personal goals.

Unhappy marriages

What happens in unhappy marriages, and those that fail?

1. Negative verbal and non-verbal acts, which are often reciprocated. This has been described as 'negative reciprocity' – one person says something horrid and the partner replies in a similar way.

2. They are not able to solve disagreements in a peaceable manner, resulting in rows or violence. Some unhappy couples try to influence each other by threats of punishment or withdrawal of rewards.

3. Some of the most common reasons given for marital breakdown were found in a study of 600 couples in Cleveland (Levinger, 1960). Wives complained much more about abuse, drinking and financial problems, while the husbands complained about sex (usually not enough of it) and in-laws. The situation remains similar today.

4. Marital failure is more common in lower occupational classes, especially among the unskilled or unemployed; when the couple married young; where there are no children from the marriage; the couples' own parents were divorced; the wife is working, especially when she has a good job (Gibson, 1994).

SAQ
20

Which aspects of marital behaviour could social skills training help with?

Relationships at work

Relationships at work are quite different from those with friends or family. People at work are brought together by the way the work is organized. Some are brought together as work colleagues in a co-operative relationship, and we saw earlier how important this is for mental health. Others find themselves in opposition or competition. A central work relation is between supervisors or managers and those supervised. This needs special skills, and it was one of the first kinds of social skill to be studied. Three aspects of supervisory skill have been found to maximize the effects on productivity and job satisfaction and related variables, over a variety of different kinds of work situation:

1. *Initiating structure.* This simply means telling people what to do and how to do it, and scheduling the work.

2. *Consideration.* This means looking after subordinates, seeing that their needs are met.

3. *Participation.* Authoritarian leaders give orders without explanation, which most subordinates dislike, but democratic ones consult their subordinates, and allow them to take part in decisions affecting them.

Contingencies. The need for these different aspects of supervision varies with the situation – sometimes more of one is needed, sometimes more of another.

A fourth aspect of leadership skills has recently been discovered: **charismatic leadership**. Charismatic leaders are people who can really change a group by communicating a vision or mission which inspires the members to pursue these new goals. These aspects of supervisory skills are described in another unit, *Social Influence* (Argyle, 1998).

SOMETHING TO TRY

Think of a charismatic leader. Watch him or her in action, on TV or in person. What are the verbal and non-verbal techniques which they use?

Summary

1. Studies with each kind of relationship have found differences in behaviour between those who are more or less successful or effective, for example, at making friends.

2. This information can then be used in training those who have difficulties, for example, by role-playing exercises and supplementary methods to teach non-verbal skills, verbal skills, rewardingness and so on.

3. Making friends requires some non-verbal skills (such as facial expression, tone of voice) and verbal ones (find similarities, take an interest in the other, etc.).

4. Courtship needs some extra skills, non-verbal (touch, gaze) and verbal (self-disclosure).

5. Marital training has focused on rewardingness and negotiation skills, but several others could be included, such as confirmation of other's self-image and support for their goals.

6. Supervisory skills training is widely practised, and includes teaching the use of the dimensions of initiating structure, consideration and participation.

Group Differences

KEY AIMS: By the end of Part 5 you will have learnt how the main relationships differ:
➤ *between males and females;*
➤ *at different ages;*
➤ *in different social classes; and*
➤ *in different cultures.*

The relationships which we have discussed – friends, marriage, kin and work relations – can be found at all times and in all places but they take rather different forms.

Males and females

There are thousands of studies of sex differences in relationships. A good summary of them is given by Hendrick (1988).

Friends

Women form close friendships with other women: they discuss personal problems, do a lot of self-disclosure, give each other social support, and may act as informal therapists to one another. Men do this much less, and prefer to do things together, like sport, and talk about work rather than more intimate matters; they also form groups and clubs of all kinds. The result is that for males as well as females, time spent with a female is more rewarding, and does more for loneliness (Reisman, 1981).

Kin

In general women are much more involved with the family than men are. They do more to rear the children, form closer links with their daughters, and there are similar links between sisters. It is these female–female links which hold the family together (Adams, 1995); in Britain this source of social support was once known among working class women as the 'female trade union', for example, in dealing with difficult husbands. Nevertheless the 'head of the family', who controls the finances, is usually, though not always, male.

Love and marriage

Males and females have played different roles for generations, the husband going out to work, the female doing the housework and child-rearing. This is now changing as more women go out to work, but they are still doing most of the housework. Men benefit more from marriage in terms of happiness and health and suffer more from bereavement and divorce. This is partly because wives are their mate's main confidant and source of support, while women have better contacts with female kin and friends.

Work

Women are more concerned with the social aspects of jobs, and often tend to choose jobs dealing with people, like teaching and nursing. Women in supervisory

49

positions are found to deal with their subordinates in a more caring and democratic way than men, but have difficulty in being promoted to these positions, partly because of prejudice, partly because family life diverts their energies, and in some cases because of their fear of success in male occupations (Argyle, 1989).

SAQ 21

Would you say males or females have more satisfying relationships?

Age differences

Friends

Children start by having playmates, a simple and impermanent relationship, but from eight to ten years of age they start to see the other's point of view and form more committed and lasting friendships. Adolescents feel the need for a close friend, and for a group of friends; this is important in developing independence from their parents and in identity formation. From adolescence to student age they may see their friends every day, and talk on the phone too. Adults see their friends much less often, because of time taken by marriage, family and work. Older people, who may be retired or widowed, need friends again.

Kin

Children have to see a lot of their family, and are usually quite glad to get away from them when they leave home. It has been found that there is least interest in family between the ages of 20–30, though parents and siblings are kept in touch with. In later life individuals may become dependent on kin, or live with them, and become very interested in the grandchildren.

Love and marriage

Most people marry in their 20s, often, in western society, after a period of co-habitation. Marriage is at first passionate and intense, but in later years becomes 'companionate', still committed but less emotional.

Work

Young people have to be 'socialized' into work, to learn to work under a supervisor in a group and to derive satisfaction from work. This process starts at school. For young people, the immediate co-workers and group are important, and the same is true of older workers, for whom the social contacts may become more important than the work itself.

A POSSIBLE PROJECT

Find a male and a female, aged between 40–50. Interview them to find out how much time in the past week they have spent with their friends, how many telephone calls, and how many e-mails (if any). Repeat this with two young people aged 17–20. It is expected that the young people will have spent much longer with their friends (Nicholson, 1980).

Social class

There are many studies on this topic, and a review of these can be found in Argyle (1994c).

Friends

Middle class individuals, in Britain, have about twice as many friends as working class people do, though the latter see their friends more often. Middle class people find their friends more at work, and in leisure groups, as well as from school and college. Most friends come from the same social class, though in leisure groups like religious groups there are also cross-class friendships; shared interests can override class differences. However, leisure groups are themselves stratified, each having its social niche. In a study in 'classless' Australia, Wilde (1974) located six social classes, and found that each club straddled more than one class, though the leadership was drawn from the higher class members.

Middle class people invite their friends home more, their houses being better equipped for this purpose, and friends are shared by both partners.

Kin

Middle classes see their friends more, working class people see their kin much more, once a week, daily for some. One explanation may be that working class people do not move about the country so much, in pursuit of education or jobs (Allan, 1979; Adams, 1968), so that there are often kin within walking distance.

Among the working class, major help is sought from kin rather than friends, as found by Willmott, 1987 (*Table* 5.1).

Table 5.1: Help given by friends and relations (Willmott, 1987)

	Middle class	White collar	Working class
Advice on a personal matter			
friends	64	67	39
relatives	34	33	58
Source of financial loan			
friends	26	23	9
relatives	74	73	86
Main source of help in child's illness			
friends	39	45	19
relatives	56	55	77

On the other hand there is more money transfer to children in middle class families.

Love and marriage

Working class couples get married earlier, often when the girl is pregnant (Reid, 1989). Couples can be hard up and may have to live with one set of parents

(Morris, 1990). This may explain why working class marriages are much more likely to end in divorce.

Table 5.2: Birth of children (Reid, 1989)

Class	I	II	IIIn	IIIm	IV	V
Percentage first births conceived before marriage (1980)		9	11	20	25	
Illegitimate (1983)		5	6	12	16	
Median interval between marriage and first birth (1985)		37	33	26	18	
Percentage of mothers under 20 at first birth (1977)	6	10	12	28	31	38
Mean family size (1984)	2.04	1.99	1.86	2.20	2.24	2.47

Middle class marriages are made later, and couples rarely live with parents. Middle class couples more often share their friends, their leisure activities, and access to money, and they value intimacy and partnership more. Disagreements are more likely to be settled by talk than by violence. Spouses are usually of similar social origins and it is better for the marriage if this is so; the worst prospects are when the wife is of higher social class then her husband.

Work

Middle class people have more friends from work, some manual workers have very few; some of these jobs give very little affiliative satisfaction.

Total social contacts

Several studies have tried to estimate the total social contacts for different classes. Middle class do better from friends, marriage and work, while working class do better from kin. Overall, middle class people do better here (Oakley and Rajan, 1991), which may partly explain their better mental health and greater happiness.

SAQ
22

What is the main reason for the class differences in relations with friends and kin?

Cultural differences

Friends

Friendship exists in all cultures. The main variation of note is that in several of them there are more formalized kinds of friendship. Some are established by a ceremony, as when 'blood brothers' cut their skin and rub in each other's blood. In Australia there is still a tradition of 'mates' dating from early days in the bush, where two males form a committed relationship where the other can be relied on through thick and thin. The reason for these formal kinds of friendship is to create a relationship which can be relied on, for business, for work, or under stress, as kin can be relied on.

Living in some **collectivist cultures** such as China means that people spend more time with the immediate group of friends and family. A comparison was made between the social life of students in Hong Kong and at an American university. The Chinese students had fewer social meetings a day, but these were more often with groups than with individuals, they lasted longer, were more task-oriented and involved more disclosure (Wheeler *et al.*, 1983).

Love and marriage

There are marriages in all cultures, but they can take different forms. They may be arranged by families, more than one wife may be allowed, there may be a concubine as well as a wife, or wives may have to be paid for, by 'bride price'. There have been major historical changes in marriage in Britain, towards smaller nuclear families with fewer children, wives going out to work, greater equality and more companionship. The divorce rate has also greatly increased.

Kin

In the third world kin are the main basis of relationships, and more kin are recognized than in the West. In Africa and India there are large families living in the same dwelling place. More than this, in such collectivist societies, individuals subordinate their own goals to those of the group, there is a high level of conformity and co-operation, and intense emotional attachment to the group.

Work

In some collectivist cultures like Japan the working group is very important; in Japan efforts are made by managers to keep such groups intact. In most of the world outside the USA and Europe, supervision and management are more authoritarian and directive – the new styles of supervisory skills have not yet reached there, and may not be acceptable if they do. In India it has been found that a rather paternalistic style is most effective. In Japan there is a hangover of the traditional 'oyabum-koyun' – a relationship with an older person as a kind of foster parent. The latter gives love and protection but also harsh authoritarian rule, to which there is unquestioning obedience (Bennett and Ishino, 1963). In Africa there was resistance to working under supervision for regular hours; this was not the way work was done.

SOMETHING TO TRY

Find one or two adults who were brought up in a different culture, and interview them about their relationships with kin. How many people were there in their childhood home? Do they see their second cousins? Are there regular family gatherings?

Summary

1. **Gender**. In general, women have closer friends, keep up contacts with female kin, are more cautious in love, benefit less from marriage, and value the social aspects of work more.

2. **Age**. Friendship develops with age and is often intense in late adolescence, but this age group is not so interested in kin; romantic love is for the young and changes with time during marriage; the young have to be socialized into work.

3. **Class**. Middle classes have more friends, working classes see more of kin, middle classes marry later and often more happily, and have more friends from work and leisure.

4. **Culture**. In some cultures there are formal kinds of friendship, families are larger, more kin recognized, marriages may be arranged, working groups are often very important and supervision authoritarian.

REFERENCES

ADAMS, B.N. (1968). *Kinship in an Urban Setting*. Chicago: Markham.

ADAMS, B.N. (1995). *The Family, 5ᵗʰ edition*. Fort Worth: Harcourt Brace.

ALLAN, G. (1979). *A Sociology of Friendship and Kinship*. London: Allen and Unwin.

ARCHER, J. (1996). Evolutionary social psychology. In M. Hewstone, W. Stroebe, and G. M. Stephenson (Eds) *Introduction to Social Psychology, 2ⁿᵈ edition*. Oxford: Blackwell.

ARGYLE, M. (1988). *Bodily Communication, 2ⁿᵈ edition*. London: Methuen.

ARGYLE, M. (1989). *The Social Psychology of Work, 2ⁿᵈ edition*. London: Penguin.

ARGYLE, M. (1994a). *The Psychology of Interpersonal Behaviour, 5th edition*. London: Penguin

ARGYLE, M. (1994b). *The Social Psychology of Everyday Life*. London: Routledge.

ARGYLE, M. (1994c). *The Psychology of Social Class*. London: Routledge.

ARGYLE, M. (1996). *The Social Psychology of Leisure*. London: Penguin.

ARGYLE, M. (1998). *Social Influence*. Leicester: BPS Books.

ARGYLE, M. and FURNHAM, A. (1982). The ecology of relationships: choice of situation as a function of relationship. *British Journal of Social Psychology*, 21, 259–262.

ARGYLE, M. and FURNHAM, A. (1983). Sources of satisfaction and conflict in long-term relationships. *Journal of Marriage and the Family*, 45, 481-493.

ARGYLE, M. and HENDERSON, M. (1985). *The Anatomy of Relationships*. London: Penguin.

ARKOWITZ, H. (1975). The behavioral assessment of social competence in males. *Behavior Therapy*, 6, 3–13.

ARON, A., PARIS, M., and ARON, E. N. (1997). Falling in love: prospective studies of self-concept change. *Journal of Personality and Social Psychology*, 69, 1102–12.

ARONSON, E. and WORCHEL, P. (1966). Similarity versus liking as determinants of interpersonal attractiveness. *Psychonomic Science*, 5, 157–8.

BENNETT, J.W. and ISHINO, I. (1963). *Paternalism in the Japanese Economy*. Minneapolis: University of Minnesota Press.

BERKMAN, L.F. and SYME, S.L. (1979). Social networks, host resistance, and mortality: a nine year follow-up study of Alameda county residents. *American Journal of Epidemiology*, 109, 86–204.

BERSCHEID, E. and WALSTER, E. (1978). *Interpersonal Attraction*. Reading, MA: Addison-Wesley.

BLOOD, R.O. (1972). *The Family*. New York: Free Press.

BOLGER, N. and ECKENRODE, J. (1990). Social relationships, personality and anxiety during a major stressful event. *Journal of Personality and Social Psychology*, 61, 440–9.

BOWLBY, J. (1969). *Attachment and Loss*. London: Penguin.

BROWN, G.W. and HARRIS, T. (1978). *Social Origins of Depression*. London: Tavistock.

BROWN, S.L. and BOOTH, A. (1996). Cohabitation versus marriage: a comparison of relationship quality. *Journal of Marriage and the Family*, 58, 668–78.

BRYANT, B. and TROWER, P. (1974). Social difficulty in a student population. *British Journal of Educational Psychology*, 44, 13–24.

BUI, K.-V., PEPLAU, L.A. and HILL, C.T. (1996). Testing the Rusbult model of relationship commitment and stability in a 15-year study of heterosexual couples. *Personality and Social Psychology Bulletin*, 22, 1244–57.

BUSS, D.M. (1988). The evolution of human intrasexual competition: evolutionary hypotheses tested in 37 cultures. *Behavioural and Brain Sciences*, 12, 1–49.

BUSS, D.M., LARSEN, R.J., WESTEN, D. and SEMMELROTH, J. (1992). Sex differences in jealousy: evolution, physiology and psychology. *Psychological Sciences*, 3, 251–5.

BUUNK, B.P. and VAN YPEREN, N.W. (1991). Referential comparisons, relational comparisons, and exchange orientation: their relation to marital satisfaction. *Personality and Social Psychology Bulletin*, 17, 710–18.

BYRNE, D. (1971). *The Attraction Paradigm*. New York: Academic Press.

CAMPBELL, A. (1981). *Girl Delinquents*. Oxford: Blackwell.

CAMPBELL, A., CONVERSE, P.E. and ROGERS, W.L. (1976). *The Quality of American Life*. New York: Russell Sage.

CARTER, H. and GLICK, P.C. (1970). *Marriage and Divorce: A Social and Economic Study*. Cambridge, Mass.: Harvard University Press.

CLARK, M.S. and MILLS, J. (1979). Interpersonal attraction in exchange and communal relationships. *Journal of Personality and Social Psychology*, 37, 12–24.

COCHRANE, R. (1988). Marriage, separation and divorce. In S. Fisher and J. Reason (Eds), *Handbook of Life Stress, Cognition and Health*. Chichester: Wiley.

COLLINS, N.L. and READ, S.J. (1990). Adult attachment, working models, and relationship quality in dating couples. *Journal of Personality and Social Psychology*, 58, 644–63.

DAWKINS, R. (1976). *The Selfish Gene*. Oxford: Oxford University Press.

DESTENO, D.A. and SALOVEY, P. (1996). Jealousy and the characteristics of one's rival: a self-evaluation maintenance perspective. *Personality and Social Psychology Bulletin*, 22, 920–32.

DUTTON, D.G. and ARON, A.P. (1974). Some evidence for heightened sexual attraction under conditions of high anxiety. *Journal of Personality and Social Psychology*, 30, 510–7.

ELLIS, A. and BEATTIE, G. (1976). *The Psychology of Language and Communication*. London: Weidenfeld and Nicholson.

EREL, O. and BURMAN, B. (1995). Interrelatedness of marital relations and parent–child relations: a meta-analytic review. *Psychological Bulletin*, 118, 108–32.

ETZIONI, A. (1961). *A Comparative Analysis of Complex Organizations*. Glencoe, Ill.: Free Press.

EYSENCK, H.J. and EYSENCK, M.W. (1985). *Personality and Individual Differences*. London: Routledge and Kegan Paul.

FEINGOLD, A. (1992). Good-looking people are not what we think. *Psychological Bulletin*, 111, 304–41.

FESTINGER, L., SCHACHTER, S. and BACK, K. (1950). *Social Pressures in Informal Groups: A Study of a Housing Community*. New York: Harper.

FITZPATRICK, M.A. (1984). A typological approach to marital interaction: recent theory and research. In L. Berkowitz (Ed) *Advances in Experimental Social Psychology*, 18, 2–47.

FRENCH, J.R.P. and RAVEN, B. (1949). The bases of social power. In D. Cartwright (Ed) *Studies in Social Power*. Ann Arbor, MI: University of Michigan Press.

FURNHAM, A. and ARGYLE, M. (1998). *The Psychology of Money*. London: Routledge.

GIBSON, C. (1994). *Dissolving Wedlock*. London: Routledge.

GUPTA, U. and SINGH, P. (1982). Exploratory study of love and liking and types of marriages. *Indian Journal of Applied Psychology*, 19, 92–7.

HAYS, R.B. (1985). A longitudinal study of friendship development. *Journal of Personality and Social Psychology*, 48, 909–24.

HAZAN, C. and SHAVER, P.R. (1987). Romantic love conceptualized as an attachment process. *Journal of Personality and Social Psychology*, 59, 511–24.

HENDRICK, C. (1988). Roles and gender in relationships in S. Duck (Ed) *Handbook of Personal Relationships*. Chichester: Wiley.

HOFFMAN, L.W. and MANIS, J.D. (1982). The value of children in the United States. In F.I. Nye (Ed) *Family Relationships*. Beverly Hills, CA: Sage.

HOLLANDER, E.P. (1985). Leadership and power in G. Lindzey and E. Aronson (Eds) *Handbook of Social Psychology*, 3rd edition. New York: Random House.

HOMANS, G.C. (1950). *The Human Group*. London: Routledge and Kegan Paul.

HORWITZ, K.A.S., WHITE, H.R. and HOWELL-WHITE, S. (1996). Becoming married and mental health: a longitudinal study of a cohort of young adults. *Journal of Marriage and the Family*, 58, 895–907.

HOUSE, J.S. (1981). *Work Stress and Social Support*. Reading, Mass.: Addison-Wesley.

HUSTON, T.L., SURRA, C.A., FITZGERALD, N.M., and CATE, R.M. (1981). From courtship to marriage: mate selection as an interpersonal process. In S. Duck and R. Gilmour (Eds) *Personal Relationships,2.Developing Personal Relationships*. London: Academic Press.

INGLEHART, R. (1990). *Culture Shift in Advanced Industrial Society*. Princeton, NJ: Princeton University Press.

JAMES, W.A. (1983). Decline in coital rates with spouses' ages and duration of marriage. *Journal of Biosocial Science*, 15, 83–7.

JARVIS, G.K. and NORTHCOTT, H.C. (1987). Religion and differences in morbidity and mortality. *Social Science and Medicine*, 25, 813–24.

JENNINGS, H.H. (1950). *Leadership and Isolation*. New York: Longmans Green.

JOURARD, S.M. (1971). *Self-Disclosure*. New York: Wiley-Interscience.

KATZ, D., MACCOBY, N., GURIN, G. and FLOOR, L.G. (1951). *Productivity, Supervision and Morale Among Railroad Workers*. Ann Arbor, MI: University of Michigan, Survey Research Center.

KELLERMAN, J., LEWIS, J., and LAIRD, J.D. (1989). Looking and loving: the effects of mutual gaze on feelings of romantic love. *Journal of Research in Personality*, 23, 145–61.

KENRICK, D.T., SALALLA, E.K., GROTH, G. and TROST, M.R. (1990).Evolution, traits, and the stages of human courtship: qualifying the parental investment model. *Journal of Personality*, 58, 97–116.

KENNEDY, S., KIECOLT-GLASER, J.K. and GLASER, R. (1990). Social support, stress, and the immune system. In B.R. Sarason, I.G. Sarason, and G.R. Pierce (Eds), *Social Support: an Interactional View*. New York: Wiley.

LARSON, R.W. (1990). The solitary side of life: an examination of the time people spend alone from childhood to old age. *Developmental Review*, 10, 155–83.

LEVINGER, G. (1966). Sources of marital dissatisfaction among applicants for divorce. *American Journal of Orthopsychiatry*, 36, 803–7.

LEVITT, M.J., SILVER, M.E. and FRANCO, N. (1996). Troublesome relationships: a part of human experience. *Journal of Social and Personal Relations*, 13, 523-36.

LOTT, A.J. and LOTT, B.E. (1974). The role of reward in the formation of positive interpersonal attitudes. In T.L .Huston (Ed) *Foundations of Interpersonal Attraction*. New York: Academic Press.

LYNCH, J.J. (1977). *The Broken Heart*. New York: Basic Books.

MARSH, P., HARRE, R. and ROSSER, E. (1978). *The Rules of Disorder*. London: Routledge and Kegan Paul.

McCLELLAND, D.C. (1987). *Human Motivation*. Cambridge: Cambridge University Press.

MORI Survey (1983). London: Market Opinion and Research International.

MORRIS, L. (1990). *The Working of the Household*. Oxford: Polity Press.

MURRAY, S.L. and HOLMES, J .G. (1997). A leap of faith? Positive illusions in romantic relationships. *Personality and Social Behavior Bulletin*, 23, 586–604.

NEWCOMB, T.M. (1961). *The Acquaintance Process*. New York: Holt, Rinehart and Winston.

NICHOLSON, J. (1980). *Seven Ages*. London: Fontana.

OAKLEY, A. and RAJAN, L. (1991). Social class and social support: the same or different? *Sociology*, 25, 31–59.

PENNEBAKER, J.W. (1989). Confession, inhibition and disease. *Advances in Experimental Social Psychology*, 22, 211–44.

RAVEN, B.H. and HALEY, R.W. (1980). Social influence in a medical context. In L. Bickman (Ed) *Applied Social Psychology Annual, Vol. I*. Beverly Hills, CA: Sage.

REICH, J.W. and ZAUTRA, A. (1981). Life events and personal causation: some relationships with satisfaction and distress. *Journal of Personality and Social Psychology*, 41, 1002–12.

REID, I. (1989). *Social Class Differences in Britain, 3rd edition*. London: Fontana.

REISMAN, J. (1981). Adult friendships. In S. Duck and R. Gilmour (Eds) *Personal Relationships. 2. Developing Personal Relationships*. London: Academic Press.

RODIN, J. and JANIS, I.L. (1979). The social power of health care practitioners as agents of change. *Journal of Social Issues*, 35 (1), 60–80.

ROOK, K. (1988). Towards a more differentiated view of loneliness. In S. Duck (Ed) *Handbook of Personal Relationships*. Chichester: Wiley.

RUBIN, Z. (1970). *Liking and Loving*. New York: Holt, Rinehart and Winston.

RUSSELL, D., PEPLAU, L.A. and CUTRONA, C.E (1980). The revised UCLA Loneliness Scale: concurrent and discriminant validity evidence. *Journal of Personality and Social Psychology*, 39, 472–80.

SARASON, I.G. and SARASON, B.R. (Eds) (1985). *Social Support: Theory, Research and Applications*. Dordrecht: Nijhoff.

SCHERER, K.R., WALLBOTT, H.G. and SUMMERFIELD, A.B. (1986). *Experiencing Emotion*. Cambridge: Cambridge University Press.

SEGAL, M.W. (1974). Alphabet and attraction: an obtrusive measure of the effect of propinquity in a field setting. *Journal of Personality and Social Psychology*, 30, 654–7.

STRAUS, M., GELLES, R. and STEINMETZ, S. (1987). *Behind Closed Doors: Violence in the American Family*. New York: Doubleday.

STRAUS, W. and STROEBE, M.S. (1987). *Bereavement and Health*. Cambridge: Cambridge University Press.

STROEBE, W., STROEBE, M. and ABAKOUMKIN, G. (1996). The role of loneliness and social support in adjustment to loss: a test of attachment versus stress theory. *Journal of Personality and Social Psychology*, 70, 1241–9.

TESSER, A. and CAMPBELL, J. (1980). Self-definition: the impact of the relative performance and similarity of others. *Social Psychology Quarterly*, 43, 341–7.

THIBAUT, J.W. and KELLEY, H.H. (1959). *The Social Psychology of Groups*. New York: Wiley.

VON DRAS, D.D. and SIEGLER, I.C. (1997). Stability in extraversion and aspects of social support at midlife. *Journal of Personality and Social Psychology*, 72, 233–41.

WALKER, C. (1977). Some variations in marital satisfaction. In R. Chester and J. Peel (Eds) *Equalities and Inequalities in Family Life*. London: Academic Press.

WARR, P.B. (1965). Proximity as a determinant of positive and negative sociometric choice. *British Journal of Social and Clinical Psychology*, 4, 104–9.

WALSTER, E., ARONSON, V., ABRAHAMS, D. and ROTTMAN, L. (1966). The importance of physical attractiveness in dating behavior. *Journal of Personality and Social Psychology*, 4, 508–16.

WALSTER, E. and WALSTER, G.W. (1978). *A New Look at Love*. Reading, MA: Addison-Wesley.

WEISS, R.S. (1973). *Loneliness: the Experience of Emotional and Social Isolation*. Cambridge, MA: MIT Press.

WELLMAN, B. (1979). The community question: the intimate networks of East Yorkers. *American Journal of Sociology*, 8, 1201–31.

WHEELER, L., REIS, H. and NEZLEK, J. (1983). Loneliness, social interaction, and sex roles. *Journal of Personality and Social Psychology*, 45, 943–53.

WICKRAMA, K.A.S., LORENZ, F.O., CONGER, R.D. and ELDER, G.H. (1997). Marital quality and physical illness: a latent growth curve analysis. *Journal of Marriage and the Family*, 59, 143–55.

WILDE, R.A. (1974). *Bradstow: A Study of Status, Class and Power in a Small Australian Town*. Sydney: Angus and Robertson.

WILLMOTT, P. (1987). *Friendship Networks and Social Support*. London: Policy Studies Institute.

WINSTEAD, B.A., DERLEGA, V.J. and MONTGOMERY, M.J. (1995). The quality of friendships at work and job satisfaction. *Journal of Social and Personal Relationships*, 12, 199–205.

YOUNG, M., BENJAMIN, B., and WALLIS, C. (1963). Mortality of widowers. *Lancet*, 2, 454-6.

YOUNG, M. and WILLMOTT, P. (1973). *The Symmetrical Family*. London: Routledge and Kegan Paul.

FURTHER READING

ARGYLE, M. (1992). *The Social Psychology of Everyday Life*. London: Routledge. Reviews research on the social causes of happiness and social and physical health.

ARGYLE, M. (1994). *The Psychology of Interpersonal Behaviour*, 5th edition. London: Penguin. Contains an account of the basic processes of making friends, and the skills needed.

ARGYLE, M. (1994). *The Psychology of Social Class*. London: Routledge. Extensive review of class differences.

ARGYLE, M.. and HENDERSON, M. (1985). *The Anatomy of Relationships*. London: Penguin. Contains an account of research on all the main relationships.

DUCK, S. (Ed.) (1988). *Handbook of Personal Relationships*. Chichester: Wiley. Handbook covering the main relationships.

HENDRICK, C. (1988). Roles and gender in relationships. In S. Duck (Ed.) *Handbook of Personal Relationships*. Chichester: Wiley. Reviews the research on gender differences.

HOLLIN, C.R. and TROWER, P. (Eds) (1986). *Handbook of Social Skills Training*. Oxford: Pergamon. Has chapters on the skills needed for a range of relationships.

LYNCH, J.J. (1977). *The Broken Heart*. New York: Basic Books. Classic book on the effect of loss of relationships on heart disease.

SABINI, J. (1992). *Social Psychology*. New York: Norton. Chapters 14 and 15 give a very readable textbook account of interpersonal attraction.

ANSWERS TO SELF-ASSESSMENT QUESTIONS

SAQ 1 Friends are people outside the family whom we like, whose company we enjoy, especially for leisure, and who are helpful and supportive.

SAQ 2 Proximity may have a negative effect if another person is unrewarding, or too different in interests, values and background.

SAQ 3 Laboratory experiments have found that participants think they would like those with similar opinions or interests, and this has been confirmed in field experiments.

SAQ 4 Three possible reasons could be: to provide practical help, to enjoy companionship, and to obtain emotional support when under stress.

SAQ 5 Skills demonstrated: paying compliments, talking about pleasant topics, agreeing, use of name, being helpful, looking for similarities, asking questions (but not too personal ones), self-disclosure. Missing are: finding common interests, humour, and, of course, positive non-verbal signals.

SAQ 6 It fails to explain that exchanges of rewards are not necessary in close, communal relationships, where members are more concerned for the other's welfare; they may also be concerned about equity as well as exchanges.

SAQ 7 Romantic attraction is more likely when individuals are emotionally aroused, when they have been socialized into knowledge of love, and when they are young, when women are attractive, and men strong and rich.

SAQ 8 The course of love is often sudden or stormy, while that of friendship is more gradual.

SAQ 9 In our own culture marriages may be traditional, dual career, or independent; in other cultures there may be arranged marriages, and men may have more than one wife.

SAQ 10 Marriages are very satisfying because of the rewards of sex, and because this relationship provides more practical help, emotional support and companionship than any other.

SAQ 11 (1) 25%, (2) 50%, (3)25%, (4) almost none.

SAQ 12 Work relations are different in being based on the organization of work, and role relations within the working organization.

SAQ 13 Being a supervisor is difficult because it means controlling subordinates by means of power, which may cause resentment and hostility, and supervisors enjoy better salary and conditions which may cause envy.

SAQ 14 Friendship and love make people happy because this raises their self-esteem, the reception of positive non-verbal signals causes joy, friends and partners do very enjoyable things together, which in the case of love includes sexual activity.

SAQ 15 A social relationship is said to buffer stress if it has a positive effect when stress occurs, but has no effect otherwise.

SAQ 16 Relationships can affect health by enforcing better 'health behaviour', and by activating the immune system.

SAQ 17 Bereavement is distressing because of the loss of a major source of social support, companionship and help, and because other relationships cannot fully substitute for the lost one.

SAQ 18 Join a club in your neighbourhood, sign up for some social skills training, read this book carefully.

SAQ 19 *Non-verbal*: gaze, touch, care of appearance, positive facial expressions. *Verbal*: find common interests, take an interest in the other person, self-disclosure but work through disagreements.

SAQ 20 Rewardingness, verbal and non-verbal, working through disagreements by discussion and compromise.

SAQ 21 Women have more intimate relations with friends and kin, men have companionship with friends and are more involved with work relations.

SAQ 22 Working class people are often less geographically mobile so keep in close touch with kin; middle class people make more friends at work and in leisure groups.

SAQ 23 In collectivist cultures, more time is spent with immediate family and friends, and goals are subordinated to those of the group. Many collectivist cultures are in the third world, and here kin are very important. Larger groups of kin live together, more kin are recognized and accept obligations to each other.

GLOSSARY

affiliation, need for: the need to be with people and have positive relations with them.

anxious/avoidant attachment: when babies show little distress if left by mother or caretaker, and little interest when mother/caretaker returns.

attachment: close relation between infant and parent, and later between loving couples, where there is distress at the other's absence or loss.

bogus stranger technique: the method used by Byrne in which participants are asked how much they would like a number of imaginary individuals who have different degrees of similarity on a number of attitude items.

buffering: a relationship preventing anxiety or other negative states when there is a stressor, but not affecting this state in the absence of stress.

charismatic leader: a leader who can inspire his or her followers to pursue a new goal or vision, especially in a time of crisis.

class, social: a division of society, seen as a social hierarchy. Usually measured in Britain by occupation, where professional occupations score 1 and unskilled occupations or being unemployed scores 5.

collectivist cultures: where great importance is attached to the group, to which individual goals are subordinated. The group may be primarily the family as in China, or the working group, as in Japan.

communal relationships: close relationships, such as love and family, where there is concern with the needs and welfare of the other.

confederates, stooges: experimental assistants who pretend to be other participants, but who have been instructed to behave in some special way.

consideration: a dimension of supervisory style, which emphasizes looking after the group and its members.

direction of causation: establishing whether variable X is a cause of variable Y or vice versa; if there is a correlation between X and Y this may be unclear. If there is an experiment, the manipulated variable can be regarded as the cause.

emotional loneliness: this is the kind of loneliness which is due to lack of a close relationship, such as that with a spouse or other partner, according to Weiss.

equity theory: the theory that partners in a relationship want to get rewards out of it in proportion to what they contribute.

exchange relationship: a relationship in which those concerned expect equal exchange of rewards, as in business relations or superficial friendships, according to Margaret Clark. Contrast with **communal relationship**.

exchange theory: the theory that people seek the maximum benefits and minimum costs in a relationship, become dependent on each other, and will expect to get equal rewards.

extraversion: the personality dimension which describes individuals who seek and enjoy social activity, as well as physical activity and other sources of high arousal.

health behaviour: behaviour that contributes to good health, such as not drinking much, not smoking, good diet, and exercise.

immune system: part of human physiology which protects the body against bacteria, viruses, etc. Often measured from immunoglobulin in the saliva.

initiating structure: the dimension of supervisory style which includes organizing the work, instructing and motivating workers, and maintaining standards of performance.

longitudinal studies: investigations where data is collected over time, so that it is possible to infer causal influences.

meta-analysis: re-analysis of a number of studies on the same issue, recalculating, where necessary, to show them in a standard form, for example, as correlations, and computing an overall measure of the strength of the relationship.

physiological arousal: heightened heart rate, blood pressure, and other autonomic indicators, as a result of fear, stress, sex or other factors.

proximity: closeness of others, spatially, or by location of residence or work place, or settings which produce frequent interaction.

regression coefficient: this is in the form of a correlation and shows the independent effect of one variable, A, on another variable, B, when the effects of other variables on A have been removed.

reinforcement: reward by food, money, praise, and so on, which is contingent on some behaviour on the part of the person reinforced.

rewardingness: the personality dimension which describes individuals who are very rewarding to others, by being helpful, friendly, and so on.

role-playing: a form of social skills training in which a trainee is asked to carry out some social task, such as interviewing or getting to know, either a confederate or other trainees. The performance is often video-taped, and this is played back as part of the later feed-back from the trainer.

role relationships: relationships, like teacher–pupil and doctor–patient, which depend greatly on the positions in an organization of those concerned.

rules, social: behaviour which is demanded by members of a group. Rules are stronger than norms, since breaking rules leads to social chaos, as breaking the rule of the road does.

rules of disorder: the rules which have been found to operate in disorderly situations like football crowds.

secure attachment: the form of attachment of babies who want to stay close to their mother or caregiver, can explore when she is present, are upset when she leaves, and are very pleased when she returns.

self-disclosure: revealing intimate information about the self to another, for example, about sex life, family or money.

self-presentation: influencing the impressions formed by others by non-verbal means like clothes and accent, or verbal ones, like name-dropping, or reported successes.

social construction: a concept, and set of ideas, which has been created in a culture, may be learned during socialization, and can affect behaviour. Romantic love is an example in the western world.

social loneliness: the form of loneliness due to lack of a network of friends or neighbours, according to Weiss.

social skills: styles of social behaviour which successfully influence the behaviour or reactions of others in a desired way

social support: helping a person in a state of distress, by being a sympathetic listener, trying to solve their problem, or by companionship.

sociobiology: the explanation of human social behaviour by its similarities with animals, and the use of evolutionary theory.

socio-technical system: the way in which different workers and equipment are related in the arrangement of the work.

trajectories, of relationships: the history of the rise and fall of relationships in terms of closeness, based on longitudinal data or recall of the history of relationships.

ACKNOWLEDGEMENTS

Table 1.1 From Wellman, B. © 1979, The community question: the intimate networks of East Yorkers, *American Journal of Sociology*, 8, pp 1201–31. Reproduced by kind permission of the University of Chicago Press.

Table 1.2 From Argyle, M. and Furnham, A., The ecology of relationships: choice of situation as a function of relationship. *British Journal of Social Psychology*, 21, 259–262, © 1982.

Table 1.3 From Willmott, P., *Friendship Networks and Social Support*. © 1987 The Policy Studies Institute, London.

Table 1.4 From Willmott, P., *Friendship Networks and Social Support*. © 1987 The Policy Studies Institute, London.

Table 1.5 From Argyle. M, and Henderson, M., *The Anatomy of Relationships*. © 1985, Penguin Books.

Table 1.6 From Ellis, A. and Beattie, G., *The Psychology of Language and Communication*. © 1976, Weidenfeld and Nicolson, London.

Table 1.7 From *Journal of Personality and Social Psychology*, 39, Russell, D., Peplau, L.A. and Cutrona, C.E., The revised UCLA Loneliness Scale: concurrent and discriminant validity evidence, © 1980. Reproduced by kind permission of the American Psychological Association and Dr Letitia Anne Peplau.

Figure 1.1 © Lesley Howling, Barnaby's Picture Library.

Figure 1.2 From Festinger, L., Schachter, S., and Back, K. *Social Pressures in Informal Groups: A study of a housing community*. © 1950, Harper-Collins, New York.

Figure 1.3 From Byrne, D, *The Attraction Paradigm*. © 1971, Academic Press, New York.

Figure 1.4 From Argyle, M. and Furnham, A., Sources of satisfaction and conflict in long-term relationships. *Journal of Marriage and the Family*, 45, 481–493, © 1983.

Figure 1.5 From Buunk, B.P. and Van Yperen, N.W., *Personality and Social Psychology Bulletin*, 17, Referential comparisons, relational comparisons, and exchange orientation: their relation to marital satisfaction, pp 710–18, ©1991 Sage Publications. Reproduced by kind permission of Sage Publications, Inc.

Table 2.1 From Rubin, Z., *Liking and Loving*. © 1970, Holt, Rinehart and Winston, New York.

Table 2.2 From Inglehart, R, *Culture Shift in Advanced Industrial Society*. © 1990, Princeton University Press, Princeton, NJ.

Table 2.3 From Argyle, M. and Furnham, A., The ecology of relationships: choice of situation as a function of relationship. *British Journal of Social Psychology*, 21, 259–262, © 1982.

Table 2.4 From Social Trends, 1986, p 36.

Table 2.5 From Argyle. M, and Henderson, M., *The Anatomy of Relationships*. © 1985, Penguin Books.

Figure 2.1 From Adams, B.N., *The Family, 5th edition*. © 1995, Harcourt Brace, Fort Worth.

Figure 2.2 From the *Indian Journal of Applied Psychology*, 19, Gupta, U. and Singh, P., Exploratory study of love and liking and types of marriages, pp 92–7, ©1982.

Table 3.1 From Campbell, A., Converse, P. E., and Rogers, W.L., *The Quality of American Life*. © 1976, Russell Sage Foundation, New York.

Table 3.2 From Brown, G.W. and Harris, T. (1978), *Social Origins of Depression*, Tavistock Publications. Reproduced by kind permission of Tavistock Publications.

Table 3.3 From Cochrane, R., Marriage, separation and divorce. In S. Fisher and J. Reason (Eds) *Handbook of Life Stress, Cognition and Health*. © 1988, Wiley, Chichester.

Table 3.4 From *Marriage and Divorce* by Hugh Carter and Paul C. Glick. Copyright © 1970, 1976 by the President and Fellows of Harvard College. Reprinted by permission of Harvard University Press.

Table 3.5 From Stroebe, W. and Stroebe, M.S. *Bereavement and Health*. © Cambridge University Press, 1987. Reproduced by kind permission.

Figure 3.1 From *Developmental Review*, 10, Larson, R.W., The solitary side of life: an examination of the time people spend alone from childhood to old age, pp 155–83, © 1990.

Figure 3.2 From Walker, C., Some variations in marital satisfaction. In R. Chester and J. Peel (Eds), *Equalities and Inequalities in Family Life*. © 1977, Academic Press, London.

Figure 3.3 From Argyle, M., *The Social Psychology of Leisure*. © 1996, Penguin Books.

Figure 3.4 From *Journal of Personality and Social Psychology*, 61, Bolger, N. and Eckenrode, J. , Social relationships, personality and anxiety during a major stressful event, pp 440–9,© 1990. Reproduced by kind permission of the American Psychological Association and Dr Niall Bolger.

Figure 3.5 From James S. House, *Work Stress and Social Support*, © 1981 (Addison Wesley). Reproduced by kind permission.

Figure 3.6 From the *American Journal of Epidemiology*, 109, Berkman, L.G. and Syme, S.L., Social networks, host resistance, and mortality: a nine year follow-up study of Alameda county residents, pp 186–204, © 1979.

Figure 3.7 From Young, M., Benjamin, B., and Wallis, C. , Mortality of widowers, *Lancet*, 2, pp 454–6, © The Lancet Ltd, 1963. Reproduced by kind permission.

Table 5.1 From Willmott, P., *Friendship Networks and Social Support*. © Policy Studies Institute, London, 1987. Reproduced by kind permission.

Table 5.2 From Reid, I., *Social Class Differences in Britain, 3rd edition*. © Fontana, 1989. Reproduced by kind permission of HarperCollins Publishers.